Resumes! Resumes! Resumes!

Third Edition

By
the editors of Career Press

CAREER PRESS
3 Tice Road
P.O. Box 687
Franklin Lakes, NJ 07417
1-800-CAREER-1
201-848-0310 (NJ and outside U.S.)
FAX: 201-848-1727

RESUMES! RESUMES! RESUMES!
THIRD EDITION

ISBN 1-56414-309-0, $10.99

Editorial direction by Lisa Mohler

Cover design by Digital Perspectives

Printed in the U.S.A. by Book-mart Press

To order this title by mail, please include price as noted above, $2.50 handling per order, and $1.50 for each book ordered. Send to: Career Press, Inc., 3 Tice Road, P.O. Box 687, Franklin Lakes, NJ 07417.

Or call toll-free 1-800-CAREER-1 (NJ and Canada: 201-848-0310) to order using VISA or MasterCard, or for further information on books from Career Press.

Library of Congress Cataloging-in-Publication Data

Resumes! resumes! resumes / by Career Press editors. -- 3rd ed.
    p.   cm.
    Includes index.
    ISBN 1-56414-309-0
    1. Résumés (Employment) I. Career Press Inc.
HF5383.R4715   1997
808' .06665--dc21

97-17756
CIP

Contents

Introduction

The Best Resumes We've Ever Seen

Show me!

Even those of us not from Missouri, the "Show Me" state, live by this motto, particularly when we are learning something new or investigating how we can improve upon skills we might already have. We learn far more quickly when *shown* how to do something rather than when simply *told* how to do it.

Think about how you might try to tell someone to perform a task as simple as folding a napkin or throwing a ball if you could use words alone. It's a daunting prospect, isn't it? How much tougher that job is when the task is something as vague as resume writing!

We can fill hundreds of pages delivering good, solid advice on how you can put together the best resume for the job you're going after. After reading through the advice, you'd probably be able to compose a fairly solid picture of your experience, education and skills. But one good resume—a mere 250 or so words—can speak volumes. We're going to do even better than show you one good resume. We're going to show you *50* great resumes! We're going to give you the best resumes seen by leading recruiting and career counseling professionals in the country, and we're going to explain why they work.

If a picture speaks a thousand words, then these resumes, selected by the likes of Robert Half, founder of Robert Half International, and top executives at companies such as Drake Beam Morin, Inc., Lee Hecht Harrison and Right Associates, will speak volumes. These are resumes that have helped people land jobs. They are resumes that were remembered—in some cases years after they were originally seen—by recruitment professionals who've seen thousands of such documents.

This book, filled with what works, will *show you* the very best way to write a winning resume.

We found it very interesting at our company that, as we put the first edition of this book together, we were in the midst of searching for someone who could fill an editorial assistant position. Our ad in *The New York Times* classified section drew more than 300 responses in a week! And, busy people all, we had to cull from this stack a short list of candidates in whom we thought we should invest the time to conduct screening interviews.

So as good-hearted people who deliver job-hunting advice, we pored over *every* word of *every* resume (no matter how sloppily typed), even the ones without cover letters. Are you kidding? We did what any average, red-blooded American employer would do. We gave each resume 20 seconds to tell us one of two things: *Read on* or *toss it*.

What is it that determines this magical make or break? As professionals in the subtleties of the job market, we can definitively say, "That depends." Perhaps the resume is a seventh-generation photocopy. Maybe it renders a portrait that's fuzzy at the edges, and we expect the candidate attached to that resume to be the same way. Maybe the candidate sent the resume in an envelope that obviously came through his or her company storage room and, what's more, sent it through the employer's postage machine. Maybe we found a typo in the first line of the cover letter (while still smarting about our company name being misspelled).

Eureka!

Just what is it, then, that sets the successful resumes apart? In the case of the search mentioned here, we selected five (that's right, *five* candidates from the more-than 300 resumes that came to our offices) to interview. Looking back at them, we can make the following generalizations:

- These resumes were neat. All were printed on good stock (not photocopy paper); they were laser-printed or typeset; and they were laid out on the page clearly and attractively.

- They were succinct. Notice we didn't say "short." Such a resume talks about the candidate and his or her accomplishments with clear, concise and precise language.

- They made us feel confident. In the case of this screening process, confident we would not waste our too-precious time finding out a little bit more about these fabulous five.

- They demonstrated that the job applicants had the right educations and experiences. They showed a clear sense of purpose and pride.

The changing market

It's probably no news to you that the job market is constantly changing and uncertain. It wasn't long ago that the country had a surplus of jobs. More recently, companies began "right sizing," and many employees found themselves consulting outplacement agencies. Those who held onto their jobs were afraid to leave them—they didn't have much confidence they would find anything else.

Today the outlook is brighter. The job market is picking up, and along with it, opportunities. Perhaps your dream job isn't available right now, but there may be other positions out there that can provide you with additional experience...and take you one step closer to that ideal career. If you feel you've reached a dead end or are ready for a change, you may want to take a realistic look at how you can transfer your skills to another, faster-growing or emerging field.

Whether jobs are scarce or plenty, your resume must deliver in form and function. Your goal is to convince the employer to spend more time with you. You need a resume that looks good and clearly reveals what you have to offer.

If you're fortunate enough to have more than one possibility, or are up against only a few other candidates, that doesn't mean you can sit back and rest on your laurels. Your resume still must pass that 20-second time test. You could be the most experienced applicant, but if you don't make a positive first impression, employers will look elsewhere.

What this book will teach you

As the old saying goes, nothing succeeds like success. The resumes in this book are winners. They landed candidates jobs and were remembered— sometimes many years later—by some of the most successful and well-known recruiters, outplacement firms, personnel agencies and career experts in the country. Standing out in such a way surely will get your resume over the 20-second hurdle.

However, we don't want you simply to *copy* the resumes you'll find here. So the first part of this book will provide you good, solid advice on how to think about your qualifications, skills, experience and education and put together a winning resume.

Chapter 1 talks about how you should think about your resume—as an advertisement or direct-mail piece with which you are hoping to sell *you*.

Chapter 2 talks about the various approaches you can take in writing a resume and just how to determine exactly which is the best approach for you, whether you are just getting out of school or a veteran of the work force. While this chapter strongly stresses that no two resumes should look alike, it provides some firm guidelines on items that you should *never* include.

Chapter 3 discusses the various resume formats from which you can choose—chronological, functional or combination, even electronic resumes. It also talk about the contents—what the employer really wants to know.

Chapter 4 provides more do's and don'ts so your resume will be readable, polished and professional. It also echoes the famous advice that Ernest Hemingway had for authors: Write standing up. Edit sitting down. This chapter talks about how to make yourself sound more intelligent than even *you* thought you were.

Then comes the section that puts this book in a class by itself, real-life resumes that are the talk of the recruiting establishment. We asked job hunting and career professionals for the best resumes they'd ever seen and the reasons why they stood out.

The largest section of this book delivers those resumes and explanations. Taking the advice we provide in the first section of this book and then comparing your efforts to the resumes you'll find here will help you put together a resume that will be remembered by employers with just the right job for you. Good luck!

Chapter 1

The Product? You.
The Advertisement? Your Resume!

Think for a minute about the best magazine advertisement you ever saw. Why did the marketer spend the money and the time to place that ad in front of you? What did it accomplish? Why?

First the ad made you stop and read what the marketer had to say. When you opened that copy of *Newsweek*, *Rolling Stone* or *Vogue*, perhaps the last thing you wanted to do was shop. Thanks to a picture, headline, color, layout, you stopped reading long enough to give that marketer some of your time, probably the most precious commodity today.

Time is on my side

That's precisely what you want your resume to do—buy a little time from prospective employers. Pique their interest, encourage them to give your resume a little more attention than they do other candidates'. If you can grab their interest, perhaps they'll devote more time to getting to know you better. In this light, your resume is an advertisement for *you*. It must describe you and it must suit you.

By the latter, we mean that *form* must fit *content*. You wouldn't expect an ad for Diet Pepsi to look like one for Preparation H (or vice versa). Yet, some creative directors might very well have resumes that look like bankers' resumes, and some bankers might come up with resumes that look like those of art dealers. In such cases, the form of the resume would set up a false expectation with the customer (the employer) and defeat the purpose of putting together the resume in the first place.

A resume must scream out, "This is who I am! This is what I want to do in my career!" It must intrigue the potential employer. It must convince him or her that *you* are worth further investigation.

So now you're ready to write?

Okay, describe yourself and what you want to do and there you'll have it: the perfect resume. Except it's not that easy. Getting back to our advertisement analogy, you first must develop a really good feel for the product, must sincerely believe in it, or the ad will ring false. How do you get to know yourself a little better to market yourself effectively? Take stock. Gather information about your:

- Work or internship experience.
- Education (high school, college and graduate school).
- Special training (seminars, certifications, licensing, etc.).
- Military experience.
- Volunteer experience.
- Skills.
- Awards and honors.
- Memberships and activities (professional and social).

To organize this material, use the worksheets described next and shown at the end of the chapter.

Work experience: Go on, sell 'em

Write down the most salient details of every job you've held. And that means *every* job: selling hot dogs at the ballpark as well as some high-level executive position that landed you an office with a window. If you've been working for several years or more, pay particular attention to your most recent positions, but don't dismiss part-time jobs or those you held early on in your career. First put down the nitty-gritty details of these positions, including:

- Each employer's name, address and telephone number.
- Names of supervisors.
- Exact dates worked at each company.
- Approximate number of hours per week.
- Specific duties and responsibilities.
- Specific skills utilized.
- Awards, letters of recommendation.

Take another look at what you *did* at those jobs. What's probably coming to mind are phrases like, "edited copy," "made sales calls" or "designed widgets." Will phrases like these add up to exciting advertising copy? Do Pepsi's ads merely state that it is a soft drink? In putting together your resume, it's more important to think about what you *accomplished*. Your job descriptions on this worksheet should contain phrases like these:

- Improved a computer-aided design system for refining widget plans.
- Achieved record year in Sheboygan, Wis.

Do these sound pretty good to you? Well, they should be better. You should give these accomplishments more thought. Whenever possible, state the benefits in precise, objective terms: numbers are good for providing that element of precision.

- Refined computer-aided design system that improved productivity of department 31%.

If you list a work-related award or honor, think about what's special about it. Were you one of only three people to receive it? Make it sound important to someone unfamiliar with your field. Many of you are probably thinking, "I've never accomplished *anything* on the job." We don't buy that. Look at the evaluations you've received from your superiors (you should've saved those). Think about promotions you've gotten and why you deserved them.

Think about big projects your department handled. What role did you play? What about the day-to-day job you did? How did the company benefit from having you on the payroll?

Volunteer experience

Some candidates have the mentality of an appraiser: "If something is free, it has no value." But the fact is your unpaid volunteer experience can be a gold mine for great resume marketing copy.

Whatever your volunteer experience, you can turn it into valuable "sales copy" on your resume. This is particularly valuable for people with little or no work experience or for people, such as homemakers, who are returning to the work force after a somewhat lengthy hiatus. Were you captain of the football team or president of the 4-H club? Have you been a coach of the local Little League team or involved in your church's charitable activities? This translates into valuable work-related experience.

The old saying, "If you want something done, give it to a busy person," connotes that employers love people who are "doers." Your *active* participation in volunteer organizations will show that you are such a busy person. You should note volunteer experience on a worksheet the same way you would your paid work experience. Include the following:

- Each organization's name, address and telephone number.
- Name of the paid director or the voluntary leader you worked with.
- Exact dates when you were involved in the organization.
- Approximate number of hours per week you spent doing things for the organization.
- Specific duties and responsibilities.
- Specific skills used.
- Awards, letters of recommendation.

Describe your responsibilities and accomplishments in professional terms. Think of how you can *quantify* the experience so your membership appears to be more than something you did in name only. Did you manage a fund drive? Increase membership 20 percent? Handle the budget?

If you've been a long-time member of an organization, describe your climb through the ranks the same way you would your job history. Talk in terms of *accomplishments*, rather than just deeds. This worksheet should have phrases like these:

- Helped organize the first girls' soccer team in Glen Ridge. Recruited coaches, arranged for sponsorships for six teams, gained the participation of 72 girls.
- Helped raise $50,000 for United Way's annual drive in Altoona. Recruited telephone marketing volunteers, wrote scripts, helped coordinate direct-mail effort.

Even if you never had the time to become a leader at your organization, think of the ways in which you contributed and how important your actions were to the accomplishments of the entire organization. Did you help organize the annual picnic? Create items for sale at the county crafts fair? Drive the bus for the high-school band? Don't overlook these activities that portray you as a *doer*.

Education

For those who've been working for some time, the details of academic life are relatively unimportant. However, for those on the job less than five years, education history is a critical component of the resume.

We've seen many resumes from recent graduates that were filled with what amounted to long lists of the courses they'd taken in school. But just as a listing of job responsibilities will put a potential employer to sleep, so will a listing of courses. Add a little sizzle to the steak by telling the employer what exactly you accomplished in school.

Write down these details about the high school, college and graduate school you attended:

- Name and address of each school.
- Years attended.
- Degrees earned.
- Major field of study.
- Minor field of study.
- Honors.
- Important courses.

What kind of accomplishments can you talk about in this worksheet? Well, if you maintained a 3.8 grade point average while earning 50 percent of your college expenses, that would certainly convince an employer that you are a can-do person. Or you might have won a fellowship to graduate school, been named a research assistant to a leading authority in your field of study, participated in a large number of extracurricular activities or been elected to a high post in student government.

If you did participate in many extracurricular activities, set up a special worksheet for them. Provide the following details:

- Name, address and telephone number of the organization.
- Office(s) you held.

- Duties/responsibilities with the organization.
- Number of hours you were involved in the organization per week.

Other training, military service, special skills

Did you attend courses with the American Management Association? Have you had on-the-job training from your employer in computer technology or some other specialty? Then set up a special worksheet to detail such specialized training.

If you had a stint with Uncle Sam in the military, set up a worksheet with the details concerning your tour of duty and your accomplishments.

Do you have any special skills that the other worksheets have not provided room for you to expound upon? Perhaps you speak a foreign language fluently or have a particular affinity for working with computers. Then set up a worksheet headed, "Special Skills," on which you can detail:

- Name of the skill.
- Specific training received in that specialty.
- Years of experience you've had working in the area.
- Your level of expertise.
- Accomplishments related to this skill.

To sum it all up

After you've completed all of these worksheets, summarize your various skills on yet another piece of paper. Write down the total number of years' experience you have performing particular tasks (perhaps you've been a sales executive for eight years, or, with your volunteer experience, have 14 years of experience handling a budget).

These skills should fit into areas that correspond to "real jobs in the real world" such as accounting, computer operations, management, public relations, editing, sales, marketing and teaching.

In the introduction of this book, we talked about a review of resumes that we did at our company. While we were going through the stack of hopefuls, we were not merely looking for sparkling documents, but for descriptions of candidates who would fulfill a *need* that our company had. Therefore, the best resume will tell the employer that you've got what he or she wants, that you can solve a problem. The following chapters will discuss how to engineer a resume that will do just that.

1. Work Experience

(Make one copy of this worksheet for each paid job
or professional internship position you have held.)

1. Name of company_____

_____

2. Address and phone number_____

_____

3. Your job title (Use the actual title that would be on employee records.)_____

_____

4. Start and end dates (month and year)_____

_____

5. Salary (beginning and end)_____

_____

6. Supervisor's name and title_____

_____

7. General job description (one- or two-sentence summary of your job)_____

_____

_____

_____

_____

_____

8. Responsibilities

   Management/supervisory duties (include size of staff and specific duties—hiring,
   training, etc.)_____

   _____

   _____

   _____

   _____

   Budgetary/financial duties (include any duties related to money—writing a budget,
   totaling daily receipts, analyzing cost/profit ratios, etc.)_____

   _____

   _____

   _____

   _____

   Sales/marketing duties (include specifics about product sold, type of customer base,
   advertising responsibilities, long-term marketing planning, etc.)_____

   _____

   _____

   _____

   _____

Customer service (include number of customers you served on a regular basis, plus their "status"—retail customer, executive-level clients, etc.)_____

_____

_____

_____

_____

Production duties (include amount of goods/services produced on a daily, monthly or annual basis)_____

_____

_____

_____

_____

Technical duties (include any duties that required you to use computers or other technical equipment)_____

_____

_____

_____

_____

Other _____

_____

_____

_____

_____

9. Accomplishments (include honors and awards)_____

_____

_____

_____

_____

_____

_____

_____

10. Special skills learned (computer skills, telephone sales, desktop publishing, etc.)_____

_____

_____

_____

_____

_____

_____

_____

2. Volunteer Experience

(Make one copy of this worksheet for each volunteer position you have held.)

1. Name of organization_____

_____

2. Address and phone number_____

_____

_____

3. Position/title (if no position held, simply indicate "member")_____

_____

4. Start and end dates of this position_____

_____

5. Start and end dates of your membership (month and year)_____

_____

6. Hours devoted per week_____

_____

7. Name(s) of organization president(s) or your ranking superior_____

_____

8. General description (one or two sentence summary of your job)_____

_____

_____

_____

_____

_____

9. Responsibilities

Management/supervisory duties (include size of staff, specific duties—coordinating, training, etc.)_____

_____

_____

_____

Budgetary/financial duties (include any duties related to money—writing a budget, totaling sales receipts, analyzing cost/profit ratios, etc.)_____

_____

_____

_____

Sales/marketing duties (include specifics about product sold, type of customer base, advertising responsibilities, long-term marketing planning, etc.)_____

_____

_____

_____

Customer service (include number of "customers" you contacted on a regular basis, plus their "status"—high school students, disabled adults, community leaders, etc.)__

_____
_____
_____
_____
_____

Production duties (include amount of goods/services produced on a daily, monthly or annual basis)_____

_____
_____
_____
_____
_____

Technical duties (any duties that required you to use computers or other technical equipment)_____

_____
_____
_____
_____
_____

Other _____

_____
_____
_____
_____

10. Accomplishments (include honors and awards)_____

_____
_____
_____
_____
_____
_____

11. Special skills learned (computer skills, telephone sales, desktop publishing, etc.)_____

_____
_____
_____
_____
_____
_____

3. Education
High school education

(If you have many years of experience under your belt, you need only complete questions 1-6 for high school education.)

1. School name_____

2. Address (city and state)_____

_____

3. Years attended_____

4. Year graduated_____

5. GPA/class rank_____

6. Honors (valedictorian, Top 10%, scholarship recipient, etc.)_____

_____

7. Accomplishments_____

_____

_____

8. Major courses_____

_____

_____

9. Special skills learned_____

_____

_____

Post-secondary education

(List here college, trade school and postgraduate work.)

1. School name_____

2. Address (city and state)_____

_____

3. Years attended_____

4. Year graduated and degree earned_____

5. GPA/class rank_____

6. Honors (valedictorian, scholarship recipient, etc.)_____

_____

7. Accomplishments_____

_____

8. Major courses_____

_____

9. Special skills learned_____

_____

_____

4. Other Training

(List here any additional vocational courses, on-job training, licenses or certification.)

1. Training received/license or certification earned_____

_____
2. Name of training institution_____
3. Address and phone number_____

_____
4. Start and end dates of training_____
5. Name and title of instructor_____
6. Skills learned_____

_____
7. Accomplishments_____

_____

_____

1. Training received/license or certification earned_____

_____
2. Name of training institution_____
3. Address and phone number_____

_____
4. Start and end dates of training_____
5. Name and title of instructor_____
6. Skills learned_____

_____
7. Accomplishments_____

_____

_____

1. Training received/license or certification earned_____

_____
2. Name of training institution_____
3. Address and phone number_____

_____
4. Start and end dates of training_____
5. Name and title of instructor_____
6. Skills learned_____

_____
7. Accomplishments_____

_____

_____

5. Military Service

1. Branch_____
2. Rank_____
3. Dates of service_____
4. Duties_____

_____

5. Special skills learned_____

_____

6. Accomplishments (include awards, citations, medals)_____

_____

_____

6. Special Skills

1. Name of skill_____
2. Specific training received_____

_____

3. Years of experience_____
4. Level of expertise_____
5. Accomplishments related to this skill_____

_____

_____

1. Name of skill_____
2. Specific training received_____

_____

3. Years of experience_____
4. Level of expertise_____
5. Accomplishments related to this skill_____

_____

_____

1. Name of skill_____
2. Specific training received_____

_____

3. Years of experience_____
4. Level of expertise_____
5. Accomplishments related to this skill_____

_____

_____

_____

7. Skills Summary

Skill area_____
    Years experience in this area_____
    Special training_____

_____

    Accomplishments_____

_____

_____

_____

_____

Skill area_____
    Years experience in this area_____
    Special training_____

_____

    Accomplishments_____

_____

_____

_____

_____

Skill area_____
    Years experience in this area_____
    Special training_____

_____

    Accomplishments_____

_____

_____

_____

_____

Skill area_____
    Years experience in this area_____
    Special training_____

_____

    Accomplishments_____

_____

_____

_____

_____

Chapter 2

Resume Form and Substance

Right about now, you're probably itching to sit down at the word processor or computer and start your resume. But before you do that, consider how you can create a resume that reflects the real you.

You have a wealth of options, in format and in the types of sections you can include or omit. Again, thinking of your resume as an advertisement, you should consider how the form of your resume fits what you're selling.

For instance, a product that's been on the market a long time ideally would have an ad that talks about longevity as an indication of quality and appeal. Think about the ads for Keds sneakers that position them simply as "what to wear."

However, a new kid on the block needs a totally different type of ad. Its strengths are unknown and unproven. Campaigns for such products must make a splash, but also talk about the care that went into their development. Consider the ads for Saturn cars from GM.

As we found in putting together this book, there certainly is no one right way to create a resume. Ask—as we did—dozens of experts to pick the perfect resume and you will come up with more variety than you would find on the menu of a good all-night diner.

Some prospective employees have a lot of experience to brag about; others have none. Some have worked for some of the leading companies in their field, while others have accomplished a great deal, but at relatively obscure operations. Some candidates earned B.A.s from Brown, M.B.A.s from Harvard, Ph.D.s from Wharton, while others worked to pay their expenses while attending St. Mary of the Plains.

All of these candidates will—or *should*—have quite different types of resumes. Because, after all,

there is only one resume format that's *right*. It's the one that best displays your skills and qualifications and shows the employer that there's a good fit between your qualities and his or her needs.

Don't write a resume without...

Before we discuss the various option packages available, let's talk about the resume elements that you absolutely cannot drive away without.

1. **Name, address and telephone number.** Believe it or not, we have received resumes lacking one or two of these three essentials. And we've gotten resumes on which the telephone number was wrong or the address was a post office box. To make doubly sure that you don't forget these elements, put them right at the top of your resume.

2. **Skills and experience.** This is the flesh and blood of the resume, the reason you'll be looked at carefully or passed by. Even if you are just getting out of school and about to embark on your first job hunt, include something here so that the employer will see that you've got what he or she *needs*.

3. **Education and training.** The length of this section will be in inverse proportion to the amount of on-the-job experience you have. But even if you're Bill Clinton, you'll want to have some mention of your education on your resume.

Resume options

That's it for the "must have's"—the four wheels, brakes, engine and driver's seat of your resume. But is this the resume you want to be seen around town in? Perhaps not just yet. You have several options to choose from that can be very useful in some situations.

1. Job objective

Some career counselors and human resources executives will tell you the job objective—a brief statement that tells the employer the type of job you want—is essential. Others will tell you it is a restatement of the obvious and a waste of valuable space.

Before we examine the pros and cons, let's first examine what a job objective paragraph typically should look like.

Objective: A position in a sales organization with a well-structured training program in which I can use and develop communications and administrative skills.

Those in the pro-objective camp will tell you that such sections tell employers exactly what you want and that you have a good handle on your career goals. In addition, it tells the busy recruiter or hiring manager, at a glance, exactly what position you're after (the recipient of your resume might have 10 job searches going on simultaneously).

However, the strength of the job objective is also its very weakness. Let's say you've been researching companies at which you'd love to work and saw that a position opened at XYZ Computer Solutions. While the fact is that, with a degree in computer science, you'd like to land *any* entry-level position at XYZ, you include on your resume a job objective that positions you for the technical sales representative opening you heard about.

The problem with the job objective in such a case is that, even though you know you're interested in other jobs at XYZ, the screener in the HR department won't.

Remember, also, that a resume is supposed to depict you as the person who can fill an employer's needs. But a job-objective paragraph right up front is talking about what *you* want. It would be as if Michelin said, "We hope you'll buy our tires so that we can get rich and retire at 48," rather than, "Buy Michelin to protect what you love the most."

However, there are two very specific types of situations in which it would be absolutely foolish *not* to include a job objective:

1. **When there is one job out there with your name on it.** You're absolutely bound and determined to be an editor on a newspaper's sports desk? Then go for it. State your precise objective and be as specific as possible. Will only a big-city sports desk do? Some will be impressed by your focus on a career goal. But you might be closing some doors that, eventually, would lead you to your ideal job.

2. **When it would be difficult for a potential employer to decipher your career goal** unless you spell it out. Let's suppose you're in transition, that you want to take the skills you've learned on one job and parlay them into a brand-new career. For instance, let's say you have vast experience in direct marketing, but would now like to become involved in fund raising for a nonprofit organization. Because your work history might not reflect that new interest, establish it up front. For instance, in such a situation the objective might read:

To use knowledge and experience in direct mail and telemarketing techniques and list selection to solicit donations for a nonprofit, charitable enterprise.

2. Summary of qualifications

Like a job objective, a summary of a candidate's skills appears at the very beginning of the resume, before any information is given about experience or education.

Just as the job objective option can tell an employer where you want to go, the summary of qualifications can give a very solid indication of where you've been and what you've done. It is a snapshot, a two-or three-phrase career in a nutshell. Here are a couple of examples:

Summary: Completing degree in journalism with a minor in marketing. Interned as assistant account executive with copywriting responsibilities at local advertising agency. Sold advertising space for college newspaper.

Summary: Sixteen years of editing and writing experience. Three years of experience managing advertising sales, promotion, production and circulation. Winner of the Jesse H. Neal Award for Journalistic Excellence.

These summaries can sound pretty good, but should you include one in your resume?

Again, the field of experts is divided. Some say such paragraphs are straight from the Department of Redundancy Department, that an employer should be able to formulate his or her own summary from reading about your experience and education.

That's certainly true. However, given the fact that you have to catch the busy screener's attention within 20 seconds, the summary may be a smart way to advertise.

The well-written summary has the same impact as the headline on an effective print advertisement. It will catch the screener's attention and convince him or her to read on. In a small amount of space, the summary can:

1. Let you showcase areas of expertise that match the employer's needs. If a classified ad indicates that management experience is essential for the successful candidate, put a summary at the top of your resume, which encapsulates all of the supervisory know-how you've developed.

2. Unearth some pearls that might be overlooked in the body of your resume. This is particularly the case if it is a two-page resume detailing several previous jobs.

3. Make the whole of your experience more impressive than the sum of the parts. If you are trying to showcase management expertise that you've gained in several jobs, add up your experience for the employer. State that you have "seven years of advertising sales experience" rather than hoping the employer arrives at this impressive statistic himself.

Remember that the summary is helpful only if you actually have something to sum up. If you are just entering the job market or have held your current job for less than a year, a qualifications summary will look absolutely ludicrous.

3. Volunteer experience

Some career experts would argue that including volunteer experience on your resume is strictly optional, but we would strongly disagree, *especially* if you don't have much on-the-job experience. As discussed in the last chapter, volunteer activities that enabled you to *accomplish* something, that allow you to demonstrate an important skill to a prospective employer, are key components of a complete resume.

4. Outside interests

Perhaps it's unfair for us to write about this option since we have such a visceral dislike for sentences such as "I like jazz, reading and going to museums" on resumes.

Of course, there are exceptions. If you're going for a job as a fitness trainer, your interest in aerobics and running will be of interest to a prospective employer. If you're applying for a job with a catering firm, your love of cooking will be a plus. And if you are trying to get a job as a road manager for the Grateful Dead, it might help if your resume talked about the two years you followed the band around the world.

But for the most part, let your personality and your real life come through during *interviews*. Why risk *not* getting an interview because your resume gives a prospective employer the notion that you spend your free time frivolously?

5. Awards and honors

Include only those awards that you received as a result of your work, your volunteer activities or your academic performance, and only those relevant to the job you're seeking.

Mentioning the appropriate awards will be the equivalent of a management "Good Housekeeping Seal of Approval." If a manager thinks well of you, you'll have an edge: he or she may see to it that other managers do, too.

6. Professional and social affiliations

If you hsve been in the job market a while and are committed to your career, you may have joined at least one trade association or other professional society. You risk looking uninterested in your career if you do not list your memberships in these organizations.

However, you shouldn't include organizations for which involvement for you has meant little or nothing more than paying your annual dues. If you are asked about one of these affiliations during an interview, you will have to admit that you really haven't been involved in the association at all.

Be even more circumspect about including social clubs and organizations on your resume. If you are applying for a job to a manager who is a dyed-in-the-wool Democrat, do you want your affiliation with the Young Republicans to close the door on any hope for working for him?

On the other hand, if you are trying to market the experience you've gained in working with these organizations, you may want to include them. Even in such cases, choose carefully. Avoid mentioning controversial causes unless you want to work only for people who will sympathize with your beliefs and you want to test them early.

Are these options? No way!

We began this chapter, you'll remember, with a list of the elements that you absolutely *must* include on your resume. Now, we are going to tell you about seven deadly resume sins—things you should *never* include.

1. **The word "resume."** Let's face it, you probably wouldn't want to work for anyone who couldn't recognize a resume as a resume. Don't waste space. Use it to tell the prospective employer one more scintillating detail about yourself.

2. **Salary information.** Sometimes employers specifically request "salary history" or "salary requirements" of applicants. But you should never include your income history on your resume. It can either eliminate you from consideration (if you make "too much") before you ever get in the door, or it can tell the employer that he or she can get you cheap. These are not the types of signals you want your resume to send.

3. **Job references.** Again, this is information that can be included on a separate sheet. Some people write, "References available upon request" toward the end of their resumes, but this is unnecessary. Few employers are about to hire a candidate who can't produce a good reference or two.

4. **Testimonials.** We've seen resumes that contain quotes like, "Produced an advertisement that David Ogilvy said was the best he'd ever seen." "Managing editor said that she would have worked with me forever if it hadn't been for that huge layoff."

This will do absolutely no good. After all, how much credence can such comments have when every employer knows that you wouldn't include negative comments on your resume? Or would you?

If, however, a former employer did say you were the greatest thing since work was invented, bring copies of testimonial letters along with you to the interview.

5. **Personal statistics.** In this day and age of lawsuits, it is not advisable to put information about your looks, marital status, familial status or health on your resume. Such information as, "Married, with two children. 5'11", 185 lbs. In excellent health," should not stand you in better stead with an employer, unless the employer wants to face a discrimination suit.

It's better to fill this valuable space with information about your *job* qualifications rather than with facts about your personal life that should be irrelevant to today's employer.

6. **Personality profiles.** We can't wait until we get a resume that describes a candidate something like this: "Have difficulty facing anyone before third cup of coffee. Although fun most of the time, can be moody."

It would be ridiculous to own up to such character flaws on a resume, wouldn't it? Of course. Therefore, phrases like, "excellent self-starter," "highly motivated" and, an all-time favorite, "enthusiastic," don't carry much weight.

7. **Photographs.** Are you trying to get onto the cover of *Vogue*? If so, you should send a photo along with your resume. After all, your looks are an important qualification for the type of work you're looking for.

If not, you're asking employers to do something patently illegal—make a hiring decision on the basis of looks. Do not put a prospective employer in that position—and yourself at a disadvantage—by doing something so unprofessional.

Now that we've discussed all of the do's and don'ts, it's time to discuss how you should organize all of the options you choose into an attention-getting, job-landing resume.

Chapter 3

Choosing Your Format and Writing Your First Draft

Before you begin feverishly writing your resume, hold on. You still have some more options to choose from, all of them having to do with format.

There are essentially three types of formats from which to choose:

1. **The chronological resume** organizes your employment and educational history by date (most recent first). This is usually the obvious choice for those who have been in the job market for some time. It is the format for the vast majority of resumes.

2. **The functional resume** is an expanded summary of qualifications. It devotes a great deal of space to the duties and responsibilities of all the jobs an applicant has held over the course of a career.

3. **The combination resume** is a bit of both. Some candidates with very specific jobs in mind will begin their resumes with a functional-style listing of relevant skills and accomplishments before launching into their employment histories.

In addition, **electronic resumes** are on the rise. While you'll want to organize the information for your electronic resume in one of the above three formats, there are special considerations, such as keywords, that you need to be aware of. We'll talk about those later in this chapter.

The chronological resume

There's some good news and some bad news for those electing this format. The good news: It is the "safe" choice. Most candidates use it and employers feel comfortable with this type of presentation of employment and academic information.

The bad news: It will be tough to have your resume stand out from the crowd.

Using a chronological format you would detail the various positions you've held, beginning with the most recent and working backward. For each position, provide the following information:

- Employer's name and location.
- Dates of your employment (month and year of start and end dates are sufficient).
- Position(s) held at each company.
- Responsibilities and accomplishments in those positions.

In most cases, this information comprises about 70 percent of the resume and is delivered right after the job objective and skills summary, if included. Some candidates choose to place their educational credentials first, deeming these their most important qualification for the job they are seeking.

This format is also useful for detailing volunteer experience. Simply list volunteer positions in the same manner as you would paid positions, providing the organization's name, the years of your involvement with the organization, your position and your responsibilities and accomplishments.

The chronological resume works best when all or most of the following apply:

1. You have a history of employment or volunteer work that shows stability.

2. You've been working in the same field for a while and are seeking another position in that area.

3. You have had a steady upward progression of titles and levels of responsibility throughout your working life.
4. You have not been a job-hopper and have been able to endure at least one year with every employer you've had.

The functional resume

For many people, the chronological resume spells disaster. It can shed unflattering light on a history of job-hopping and reveal a career progression that resembled a zigzagging road through hill country, rather than a ladder straight to the top.

The functional resume, on the other hand, can smooth out these rough spots. Essentially the functional resume format allows you to group accomplishments, qualifications and experience—your key selling points—together. The format can help you play up your experience in specialty areas.

As some of the career experts cited later in this book will tell you, functional resumes are not welcomed with open arms in the employment world. Some employers view them as "problem resumes" because they believe the candidate has chosen the format to hide some glaring flaws or deficiencies.

Some career experts and employers also object instinctively because the names and dates of employment are played down as if, here again, the candidate were trying to hide something.

Nevertheless, you owe it to yourself to consider the functional resume if:

1. Your work history does not exactly match your new career goals.
2. You don't have a great deal of experience related specifically to the position you seek. Hence, you want to play up some of your other strengths.
3. You have noticeable gaps in your employment history.

The combination resume

To overcome employer objections to the functional resume yet allow you to position yourself in as positive a light as possible, you may want to use a combination format—taking the best parts of both functional and chronological formats. For example, if you have little professional sales experience and you're seeking a job as a salesperson, you might want to lead off with a functional-style listing of customer-service credentials and community service accomplishments—items that will demonstrate good, face-to-face "people skills." Then you could launch into the chronological listing of employment, volunteer work and education.

The electronic resume

There's no doubt about it—technology is changing the job-search process. The Internet, e-mail, the World Wide Web, specialized computer software and scanners have opened new doors for job hunters and their prospective employers. If you're interested in using an electronic resume, you have a couple of options.

For example, you can save your computer-generated resume in text format and e-mail it directly to more than 600 major databases on the Internet. These databases represent a variety of employers and career services. Or you can have your printed resume scanned into a computer where it's saved as data and then transmitted to an employer's database. This allows you to send your information electronically rather than through the U.S. mail. Yet another possibility would be to create your own World Wide Web page.

Each of these options has its advantages and disadvantages, and what may work best for you will depend greatly on what equipment and services you have available.

But there is one thing all electronic resumes have in common: keywords. Keywords represent specific skills. To find some examples, open your newspaper to the Employment section of the classified ads. What specific skills are listed in job descriptions or requirements in your field? You've just found keywords.

Take for instance an ad for a materials engineer. You might find phrases like "packaging standards," "point of use storage," "automated material handling systems," or "bachelor's degree in material handling." If you're a materials engineer with these qualifications, use them as your keywords. The *Occupational Outlook Handbook,* published by the U.S. Department of Labor, also has keyword information and can be found in the reference section of your local library.

The employer or career service's computer software then sorts those keywords to find a match for its needs. Some candidates choose to group keywords in a separate section at the top of the page. Others sprinkle them throughout the resume. Whichever the case, be *specific*—computer software can't interpret what you mean.

For more detailed information on preparing text resumes to send via e-mail, see what experts Steven Provenzano (page 36) and Kathryn Troutman (page 134) recommend. If you'd like to create a Web resume, expert Rebecca Smith offers advice on page 82. A few last notes:

- When preparing a print resume that will be scanned into a computer, use standard resume formats, common headings and standard typefaces on white paper, printed by a laser printer. Omit all graphic devices such as boldface type, boxes, lines and shadows.

- Using this technology brings up personal and privacy issues which you may want to consider before proceeding.

- Because print and electronic resumes are so different, and not all employers use e-mail, experts advise that you have one of each.

- As with any resume, keep your electronic resume current.

The choice is yours

Perhaps the best way to determine the right format for your resume is to put yourself in the employer's shoes. Consider:

1. If you were the employer, what would you want *most* from the person you're hiring? What would be the first thing you would look for on the resume? The right degree? The right job experience? A long history in the industry?

2. What will the employer see as your very best qualifications for the job? Will it be education? Special training you have received? Proof of management expertise?

The answers to these questions will help formulate a resume that will produce results.

Writing that resume

At last! It's time to take all of the lessons learned so far in this book and begin *writing* your resume. The most fundamental rule of resume writing is that you must lead with your best foot, emphasizing the skills, the experience and the technical knowledge that will most help you get the job you want. Remember the prospective employer out there has a need, and you're out to convince him or her that you can fill it.

In resume-writing, it is essential that you make every word count. Screeners, recruiters and hiring managers you're trying to appeal to won't have the patience for long-windedness or verbal meandering. Say what you have to say clearly and concisely.

And, at least as you're putting together your first draft, don't feel that you have to be perfect. Be more concerned with communicating to prospective employers, rather than having a perfect style. You will have a chance to polish it later.

The ideal resume length?

Myth: A resume should *never* be more than one page long.

Fact: Your resume must be as succinct as possible, but long enough to adequately relay your experience and qualifications. Thus, if you've just entered the work force and your job experience is scarce, one page will probably be plenty of room for you to spell out your skills.

If you've been in the work force for several years and have accumulated a variety of valuable experiences, then by all means take two pages to communicate this to prospective employers. Don't sell yourself short by cutting out impressive qualifications to squeeze your resume onto one page.

But, as a rule, we don't recommend going over two pages. Most employers simply won't read anything longer, unless they're searching for a high-level executive. What's more, most employers think that candidates who cannot limit themselves to a two-page resume lack essential organizational and communication skills.

Yet rules are meant to be broken. And as you'll see in the second half of this book, the experts will give you a wide range of answers. For recruitment guru Robert Half, the ideal resume is short and sweet. In fact, the best resume he ever saw (you'll see it on page 151) is only *36 words* long!

However, Barbara Provus, principal and co-founder of Shepherd Bueschel & Provus, Inc., likes best the resume weighing in at *four pages* that you'll see on pages 171 to 174.

Watch your language

One way to assure your resume is not overly "windy" is to write it in a telegraph style. Don't use full sentences. Instead, begin each entry with an arresting action word, but avoid using words over and over or you'll seem terribly uncreative. Dust off your thesaurus and look for a wide variety of words to describe your responsibilities. To help you choose the best resume-*ese*, consult these words that can give power to your resume:

accomplished	counseled	gathered	obtained	reported
achieved	created	generated	operated	represented
adjusted	decreased	guided	organized	researched
administered	delivered	headed	ordered	restored
advised	designated	identified	overhauled	reviewed
analyzed	designed	implemented	performed	revised
approved	detected	improved	persuaded	scheduled
arranged	determined	increased	planned	selected
assisted	developed	initiated	prepared	served
budgeted	devised	inspected	presented	sold
built	diagnosed	installed	presided	solved
calculated	directed	instituted	processed	studied
charted	discovered	instructed	produced	supervised
compared	distributed	interpreted	programmed	supplied
compiled	edited	invented	promoted	systematized
completed	eliminated	justified	proposed	taught
composed	enlarged	lectured	provided	tested
conducted	established	led	purchased	traced
consolidated	evaluated	lobbied	recommended	trained
constructed	examined	maintained	reduced	translated
consulted	expanded	managed	referred	updated
controlled	formulated	modified	regulated	utilized
conceptualized	founded	motivated	reorganized	won
coordinated	flagged	negotiated	replaced	wrote

The chronological resume

1. The header

The header, which tells employers your name and how they can reach you, should always be the first thing on the first page of your resume. Set the header—or at least your name—in boldface type at the center of the page so that it is prominent.

Include your full name (or at least first and last name with middle initials) and, even if you've been called Rusty or some other sobriquet your entire life, don't use a nickname. Of course it's essential to include your address and phone number.

If you're employed, include daytime and evening phone numbers. If you're unable to accept confidential calls at work, include only your home number, but be sure to attach an answering machine. It's unlikely that employers will call you after office hours. If you are at a temporary address, indicate where you can be reached after a certain date.

2. The job objective (optional)

If you decide to include a job objective, include it right under the header. Set the objective off with the headline, "Objective," "Job Objective" or "Career Objective."

When writing your objective, avoid the trap that so many job seekers fall into—using vague words and phrases that really don't add up to much. If you are going to write an objective like the one below, don't bother to include one.

> To obtain a position in a progressive company where I can use my skills to increase sales and contribute to the overall success of the organization.

Instead, spell out exactly what you are looking for. Be strong, confident, focused and concise.

To direct a sales organization at a consumer products company.

To obtain a position in an architectural firm specializing in industrial interiors.

That tells the employer *what* you want to do. The rest of the resume tells the employer *how* you will do it if you're hired.

3. The skills summary (optional)

If you decide to include this element on your resume, place it directly under the header or the job objective. Set it off with a headline such as "Skills Summary," "Experience Summary" or "Summary of Qualifications." You can present this summary in a single paragraph or in a series of bulleted points.

Why are you including a summary? It *is* a good way to catch an employer's attention and make him or her want to learn more about you. But do not overdo it! If you decide on a paragraph style, use two or three short sentences. For instance:

Summary of Qualifications: Supervised account teams working on major consumer products advertising campaigns. Seven years of copywriting and creative supervisory experience. Master's in marketing.

If you wish to use bullets, include no more than four or five items. For example:

- 16 years in association management.
- Expertise in convention management, publishing and membership development.
- Winner of Innovator award from U.S. Society of Association Executives.
- Strong background in advertising, telecommunications associations.

Include your most salient strength first. If you have, say, two key strengths, each of which might be more important to different types of employers, do two resumes.

4. Experience

Experience, according to the old saying, is the best teacher. Hence it's this section of your resume that employers are most interested in and to which you should devote the most space.

The first thing to consider is whether you want to group paid and volunteer positions or list them separately. It's probably a good idea to group them if you don't have a great deal of paid experience under your belt just yet.

If you do that, a good heading for the section might be, "Professional and Volunteer Experience," or simply "Experience."

The only problem is, if you have held volunteer and paid positions simultaneously, putting them in a chronological format might confuse an employer.

Most people include only paid positions in the Experience section, then follow with their volunteer activities and memberships.

The listing of your positions should look something like this:

Gordion Wire Co., Waukesha, Wis.
Director of Research, 1990-present.
Developed strategy for company's entry into international markets. Supervised staff of two research assistants. Examined implications of foreign exchange fluctuations, various political situations and availabilities of adequate distribution channels. Findings led to company's entry into Pacific Rim.

Employees who've held several jobs with one company, thanks to promotions, have something great to brag about on their resumes. Yet most of these candidates do a very poor job of enhancing this positive selling point on their resumes. Here's the best way to present such a history:

Crown Distribution Company, La Jolla, Calif., July 1985-present.
Director of Sales and Marketing, 1992-present. Oversee sales activities of 60 representatives throughout U.S. and Canada. Direct-marketing and publicity strategies.

- Increased national sales 15 percent annually.
- Developed Clio Award-winning television advertising campaign.

Eastern District Sales Director, June 1987-June 1992. Supervised sales activities in 22 Eastern states. Personally handled all company's Eastern-based national accounts, comprising 48 percent of total revenues.

- Increased sales in territory 92 percent in four years and more than doubled market share.

Sales Executive, July 1985-June 1987. In charge of sales in Middle Atlantic region. Increased sales in territory 42 percent in two years.

- Won company's Salesman of the Year Award in 1985 and 1986.

As you can see in this example, the chronological format requires that you list your most recent position first. The more recently you've held a position, the more information you should provide.

Best for first

What you say about each of the individual listings on your resume depends on the importance and recency of the position. For the most recent positions, provide:

- Name of employer.
- Employer's location.
- Dates of employment.
- Position or job title.
- A summary of your responsibilities.
- Major accomplishments.

Be sure to provide *all* of this information for the first four to six positions appearing on the resume, or for the first seven to 10 years of on-the-job experience. Once you've done that, describe in full only those positions that strengthen your sales pitch. If you were the youngest person to be promoted to a position, or if you achieved a particularly noteworthy accomplishment, then it's worth describing some job out of the misty past. Otherwise, provide only the employer's name and location, your position and the dates of employment.

Here's the best way to present various components of your experience listings:

Employer/organization name and location. Always state the full name of the company, rather than using acronyms that might not be familiar to your prospective new employer. General Motors, for instance, should not be called "GM." However, 3M—well known by that name—should not be called Minnesota Mining and Minerals.

Dates of employment. Indicate the month and year you began and left each position. If you've been in the work force a long time and kept each of your jobs a year or more, you can consider leaving off the months.

Job title. Avoid the temptation to give yourself a promotion so you look better to a prospective employer. However, by all means, use commonly used job titles if a company you've worked for has used particularly idiosyncratic ones. For instance, if your company uses a title like "group leader," you might substitute the more commonly used "supervisor."

Description of responsibilities. Keep it brief. Sum up your major responsibilities in broad terms. Remember, you don't need to explain to a company seeking a customer service representative what a customer service representative does.

A list of your accomplishments. After you've told your prospective employer that you did the job, you have to demonstrate that you were *good* at it. After all, you're not going to be hired just because you showed up at your last job! This is the place where you should be specific. This is one of the few places on your resume where you'll be able to talk about your qualities *quantitatively*—in a way that's objective and easily understood.

What money-saving ideas have you come up with; how much did they trim expenses? By how much did you or your department exceed goals? These are accomplishments anyone can understand.

5. Education

The facts about your academic life generally follow the section about your experience. However, as we've mentioned, there are several circumstances in which the details of your student life should precede the experience section:

1. If you're a recent college graduate, list your academic credentials before any descriptions of internships and other temporary or noncareer-oriented work.
2. If you're changing careers and education is more pertinent to your prospective new position than your actual job experience.
3. If you're seeking a position in which specialized education is a prerequisite for employment.

In putting together this section of your resume, provide only basic details about your education—unless this is the only selling point you have. The resume should show:

1. Name and location of the school.
2. Date of graduation.
3. Degree and major area of study. (You can use the abbreviated terms for your degree, such as B.A., B.S., etc.)
4. Grade point average (optional).
5. Relevant and/or noteworthy awards and accomplishments.

The order in which you present this material depends on the points you wish to emphasize most. If you graduated from a very prestigious school, place the name of the school first, then your degree.

If you didn't graduate college, does that mean you should throw all of the work you did at school out the window? Of course not! State the years you attended and the credit hours you completed. If you completed a large number of hours in a particular field of study, say so. For instance:

Jasper Johns School of Visual Arts, 42 credits in commercial design courses, 1988-1991.

How true to your school?

Even if high school was one of the best times in your life, you shouldn't include this information on your resume unless you did *not* attend college or trade school.

If you were a high school dropout, but earned an equivalency degree, include that on your resume instead. If you moved around a lot during your high school years, list only the last school attended and from which you received your diploma. Include the same types of information you would for a college degree, except for area of study.

If you've been in the work force for a number of years, you needn't include the name of your high school at all. Employers will be more interested in your job experience than in any secondary schooling you might have had.

The GPA option

It is not necessary to include your grade point average if you've been in the work force for several years. The accomplishments and experience you describe on your resume should be enough to indicate to any prospective employer that you are an intelligent and hardworking individual. If you exhibited true signs of genius in college, however, include information on your resume indicating this.

A good rule of thumb, no matter how long you have been in the work force, is to show an employer your grades only if they're good enough to be proud of—a B-plus average or better. If your class ranking is impressive (top 10 percent) you might mention that or the fact that you graduated with honors. Do not use overkill in establishing your academic prowess. Your college line might look like any of these:

B.S., Massachusetts Institute of Technology, Cambridge, Mass., 1993. 3.8/4.0 GPA.
B.A., St. Mary of the Plains, Casper, Wyo., 1990. Ranked third in class of 320.
L.L.M., New York Law School, 1995. Ranked in top 10% of class.

Above and beyond

If you've had any extraordinary educational experiences—foreign exchange, a seminar course with a famous professor, a research assistant position—include them on the resume to demonstrate that you are someone who goes beyond the ordinary, accepts new and unusual challenges and has been recognized for excellence.

B.A., English, Babcock College, Lincoln, Nebraska, 1991.

Participated in seminar course given by E.L. Doctorow.

One year of foreign study at Birmingham (England) University.

6. Licensing, special training, certification

List any special training you've had and any professional licenses or certification you currently hold, using the most appropriate headline: "Training and Certification," "Special Training," "Professional Licenses," etc. If you prefer, you can group this information with your education rather than creating a separate section for it.

For licenses and certification, provide:

1. Name and type of license.
2. State or states in which it is valid, if appropriate.
3. Date acquired.
4. Number of the license, if appropriate.

For instance:

New York City Teaching Certification, special education, 1990.

New Mexico Real Estate License, 1992.

Certified Public Accountant, Alaska, 1994.

New Jersey Plumber's License 2386.

For special training, include:

1. Name of the course.
2. Name and location of the institution where you took the course.
3. Date you completed the training.

If you've had special training as part of your job experience—not run-of-the-mill seminars, but extensive programs—by all means include them on your resume. This information can be presented like this:

Special Training
Telephone Central Office Design: Completed intensive, three-month training program, New Jersey Bell Research Center, Newark, N.J., June 1992.

7. Memberships and activities

The affiliations you mention here might not have anything to do with your career, but they will show prospective employers that you are a well-rounded person capable of managing your time and taking on extra assignments.

The title you give this section should reflect its entire content. If it's a mixed bag, call it simply, "Memberships and Outside Activities." If your extracurricular activities are fairly specialized, call the section, "Professional Affiliation" or "Community Activities" to reflect that.

In this section, you should include only the organizations in which you are *now* involved. (Remember, this is not a section in which you are trying to provide experiences that will be deemed relevant to the job you're going after.)

These listings should be as brief as possible, providing only the organization name and positions of leadership you've held.

Again, it's probably a good idea not to include any controversial affiliations you might have unless, of course, they support the prospective employer's position on an issue. For instance, if you are an animal-rights activist, it won't hurt to mention that if you are seeking a position with a cosmetics company that prints "No Animal Testing" on its labels.

It's not necessary to include the location of the organization unless it is relatively obscure.

These listings should look something like this:

Fund raiser, March of Dimes,
    Bucks County Chapter

President, Susquatch Parent Teacher
    Association

If you've had many *significant* accomplishments as part of your "free-time" activities, you might want to construct or include them in a "Volunteer Activities" section rather than lengthening what is usually a brief section of the resume.

8. Awards and honors

Awards and honors received as a result of your work experience should already have been included within your experience profile. After all, why would you want to include items that speak so well of you here, near the very end of the resume?

If, indeed, you still have significant recognitions to talk about, then list them as "Awards and Honors" or "Additional Honors and Awards" (to flag the resume reviewer to look for others under your "Accomplishments or Experience" section).

You should provide the name of the award, the organization presenting it and the year in which you received it. Again, don't overdo this section. Include only awards of *significance*.

Outstanding Contribution Award, Glen Ridge Congregational Church, Glen Ridge, N.H., 1990.

Harold H. McGlinchy Award, Outstanding Performance, Montclair Theater, Montclair, N.H., 1992.

9. Hobbies and outside interests

If you can't resist including this section—despite all of the nasty things we said about it in Chapter 2—then please keep it short and simple. Try to list hobbies that employers will perceive as benefits to them. For instance, if you are applying for an interior design job, it might help if one of your hobbies is carpentry.

The Functional Resume

Most parts of a functional resume should be treated in the same manner they are in the chronological version, with the obvious exceptions of work experience and accomplishments.

Skill and experience profile

The big difference between chronological and functional resumes is that instead of listing each position you've held, along with its accomplishments and responsibilities, you divide your experience into general areas of skill and briefly state the experience, qualifications and accomplishments related to each of these areas.

Think about the skills you wish to highlight, taking into careful consideration what the prospective employer needs for the position you will be seeking.

For example, suppose you're applying for a job as a supervisor at a day-care center. What general areas of expertise would be most important? Childcare, teaching, management and general business.

Ideally, of course, you would have at least some experience, qualifications and accomplishments to list in each of these areas. That experience might come from a combination of paid jobs, volunteer positions and in-the-home responsibilities.

Under each skills category heading, you should list four or five of your most impressive accomplishments or abilities. For instance:

Childcare Experience

- Provided in-home day care for three preschoolers for two years.
- Assisted with toddler care in corporate day care center.
- Developed "child file" system that made vital medical data on day-care children easier to access and maintain.

Management Experience

- Supervised three cashiers as first-line supervisor in large discount store.
- Created employee scheduling procedure that resolved long-standing staffing conflict.
- Named Employee of the Month for designing and implementing improved inventory return system.

How'd it turn out?

Whether you've been burning to write your resume or dreading it, you probably have a good idea about what to say. The best thing to do is relax. Remember that this is your first draft, a document that *should* be subjected to several revisions. So just follow the basic rules of thumb in this and the preceding chapters, and let it flow.

Then, when you're happy with the way it sounds, read the next chapters to get a good feel for how it should look.

Chapter **4**

The Art of Designing and Editing

It's a bit frightening to know that most resumes are thrown away without a second glance. Imagine what the unfortunate candidates would do if they could see the screening process. They'd be screaming, "Hey, wait just a minute. That's my *life* on that piece of paper you just deep-sixed!" Our answer to many of these hapless candidates would be, "You should have thought about that before sending us this poorly written, poorly presented mess."

In the previous three chapters, we've dealt with format and writing style extensively. In this chapter, we will talk about the first impression your resume makes—the picture of *you* it conveys as the recruiter or prospective employer simply looks at it. The four hallmarks of a well-designed resume are:

1. It's easy to read.
2. There is lots of white space.
3. It's neat.
4. It's clean.

Send an employer a resume that obeys those four rules, and it will get at least more than a glance. Let's talk about each of these points a bit.

Easy to read. The resume presentation should be simple and uncluttered. While it shouldn't say "RESUME" at the top, its very look should communicate that it is, indeed, a resume. In order to be easily read, it should have sufficiently large type, should be on white or cream stock and should have a consistent presentation style.

Lots of white space. In the first four chapters of this book we've talked about how jam-packed with information your resume must be. By urging you to have lots of space, are we contradicting ourselves? No. In order for your readers to read your resume, they must feel *invited* to do so. Graphic designers speak about "entry points" on a page and "places for the eye to rest." Such points and places

are sufficiently wide margins, spacing between paragraphs and the space around headlines.

A crammed, cramped resume is forbidding to the reader. At least subconsciously it suggests that there's too much to read and that understanding the resume will be difficult. It also suggests that the resume writer could not decide what to leave out of the resume to give it a cleaner look. And no employer wants to hire indecisive candidates.

Neatness, cleanliness count. Have your resume professionally typeset or laser-printed. These are the *only* acceptable ways to produce resumes. Photocopies and typewritten pages are not acceptable. They will look second rate to any recruiter.

We've seen resumes with stains, resumes that have been folded after someone just finished reading an over-inked edition of the morning paper, resumes in fairly beaten-up envelopes. What does this say about these candidates? Nothing flattering. Don't be a slob when it comes to job hunting. Take the extra time—a matter of minutes really—to put your best foot forward in a well-polished shoe.

12 tips for better-looking resumes

1. **Use a serif typeface.** Serif typefaces, such as Century Schoolbook used in this book, have extra strokes on the letters. Tests always show that people find many of these typefaces easier to read. Open any textbook or newspaper or turn on your word processor and you'll see serif type. We see many resumes with sans-serif type lacking finials and doodads, and they're harder to read.

2. **Don't get too fancy.** Stick to traditional-looking typefaces. You may love the sound of Zapf Chancery Italic, but it won't look as good on your resume as Times New Roman.

3. **Choose a face and stick to it.** Leave the mixing of type to trained graphic artists. When amateurs mix typefaces on a document, the results are usually amateurish.

4. **Make sure the type is big enough.** The standard size is usually 11-"point" type, with a similar size of "leading" or space between the lines. If asked, you would say 11 over 11 Century Schoolbook.

5. **Highlight with boldface type.** While you shouldn't mix typefaces, you can make certain items—such as your name, names of organizations, employers and schools, and headlines stand out by using boldface (very dark) versions of the same typeface.

6. **Use underlining and capitalization sparingly.** At most, use such treatment on section heads. Such jarring changes of style slow a reader's eye.

7. **The same goes for italics.** Again, you shouldn't mix type styles too much at all. Also, your goal is to emphasize everything in your resume through punchy writing and proper positioning, so italics for the sake of emphasis are redundant.

8. **Don't skimp on the margins.** You should have at least one inch of white space on the top and no less than one-half inch on the other three sides of your resume. Narrow margins make your document look "choked."

9. **Use "ragged right" line breaks.** Your lines should end naturally, not requiring words to be hyphenated. This provides more white space than the box-like "justified" line endings you see in most books.

10. **Use single line spacing within listings,** and double spacing between sections.

11. **Use bullets to highlight** accomplishments, but limit the size of bulleted items to one to two lines. Bullets help you deliver a large number of selling points in a crisp, telegraph-like style. Using lengthy bulleted paragraphs, therefore, will only assure that your resume shoots blanks.

12. **Keep it simple.** Once you find a style you like, stick with it. Don't overdesign your resume or try to include every presentation style you've liked. Find the one you like best and use it throughout the document.

The second part of this book presents a wide variety of resume formats. Find one you like and try it, keeping in mind the rules delivered here.

The art of editing and rewriting

Ernest Hemingway delivered what is probably the best advice on how to write effectively: "I write standing up and edit sitting down." What he meant by that was: You should spend more time editing—changing and deleting—than you do writing.

Let's suppose you've written a rough draft of your resume. How do you go about making it better, even if you think it's pretty darn good? First look at the big changes you might have to make. Make them. Then take a look at the details and see how those can be corrected or improved.

The big picture

Here are some questions to ask yourself that might lead to major overhauls of your first crack at a resume masterpiece:

1. Have I communicated to the employer that I can fill a *need*? If your resume reads like an autobiography or a series of yearbook entries, you've missed the boat.

   Does this resume tell the employer what I can do for him or her? Does it make him or her confident that I am qualified and motivated enough to be given a chance? Have I spelled out the many benefits the employer would realize by hiring me?

2. Do my strengths come across? Have I chosen a format that highlights my pluses and doesn't suggest skeletons in the closet? Will a functional format make it seem as if I have something to hide? Will a chronological format make me look like a job-hopper?

3. Is there anything that can be removed? Does the list of volunteer activities suggest qualities that would be useful to an employer? What does my list of hobbies say about me? Have I accomplished enough in my career to have a summary of qualifications?

4. Does every element count? Is the job objective meaningful or does it sound as exciting as accounting-textbook prose? Did I put my best foot forward in the skills summary? Are all of the elements crisp and compelling?

Details, details, details

Once you have a resume that you're happy with and that meets the standards suggested by these questions, it's time to examine the details. Here's a checklist to help you through this editing process.

Name header

- Are my name, address and phone number prominently displayed at the top of the page?
- Did I use the most professional-sounding version of my name? (Frances instead of Cookie? William instead of Billy?)
- Did I include my *correct* address? If I am moving, did I indicate my future address and the date after which I can be found there?
- Did I include a phone number at which I can be easily reached or at which messages can be left? Did I include my area code? Check that numbers have not been transposed—a common mistake.

Job objective

- Have I stated it in 12 or fewer words?
- Is it focused and precise?
- Does it preclude my being considered for other positions? If so, should I draft alternative versions of my resume, with different objectives?

Skills summary

- Is it targeted to the job I'm seeking? Does it highlight the qualifications and experience most important to my prospective employer?
- Is it short and concise—two to three brief sentences or four or five bulleted points?

Experience profile for the chronological resume

- Did I include the correct starting and ending dates (month and year) for each job?
- Did I use the correct job title or a revised title, keeping with my duties and responsibilities?
- Did I include the correct names of my employers and the locations in which I worked?
- Are any of the paragraphs I've used to describe my jobs longer than five lines?

Functional and combination resumes

- Are the skill categories the most relevant to the job I want?
- Did I use business-oriented terms ("Childcare" rather than "Baby-sitting")?
- Did I include a brief chronological listing of paid/volunteer experience near the end of the resume?

All formats

- Did I use strong action words to describe contributions and achievements? (See page 25.)
- Did I eliminate "I," "the," "an" and other words unnecessary in resume writing?
- Did I use acronyms/abbreviations that might not be understood by everyone who will view my resume?
- Did I *quantify* accomplishments, rather than simply describe them? Did I talk about the amount of money I saved or by what percentage I increased sales?
- Did I use the correct name for each award and honor received? Did I state the organization that gave it and the year received?

Education

- Did I check the dates I received my degrees or attended schools?
- Did I check the name and location of each school?

Proofread again...and again

One typo can land your resume in the trash. Why blow a job because of a transposed letter or a stupid misspelling? Proofreading is impossible to teach, but we can give you some pointers:

1. Get out a ruler and read each and every line of your resume. This will force you to *slow down* your reading.

2. Don't rely solely on a spell-checker program. Such aids don't recognize the difference between "their" and "there." Run the spell-checker to catch spelling mistakes, but check your resume the old-fashioned way to look for other types of errors.

3. Read from the bottom up. We read faster when reading for sense. Make sure the resume won't make sense by reading from the lower right-hand corner backwards.

4. Don't go it alone. It's difficult to catch the errors in something you've pored over for hours or days. Have someone with "fresh eyes" give your final draft a careful read.

After you have proofread the resume, make corrections and check it again, making sure the resume is no less than perfect.

Now you know the basics—content, format and design—of how to put together a great resume. It's time to present the resumes deemed "The Best I've Ever Seen" by leading experts in the career field.

A Resume for the Classroom

A Few Formatting Tips for Teachers

"This modified 'curriculum vitae' format is the most widely accepted format for the teaching profession," says Joellyn Wittenstein of A1 Quality Resumes & Job Search Services in Buffalo Grove, Ill.

Why? The format immediately gives the reader a quick summary of the candidate's academic credentials and certification, essential information for those doing the hiring. Jane Wilson is looking for a special education teacher's position and therefore lists her certification in working with mentally handicapped children and those with learning disabilities. A Profile section is used to summarize her qualifications and her general scope of classroom experience.

Jane then follows with information about her teaching and related experience. Finally, bullets placed in front of sentences make this resume easy to read.

Joellyn Wittenstein, CPRW
A1 Quality Resumes & Job Search Services

Joellyn Wittenstein has been writing resumes since 1988 and opened her own business in 1991. She is a member of the Professional Association of Resume Writers, the National Association for Job Search Training and is an accredited Certified Professional Resume Writer (CPRW). Her work has been featured in David Nobles' "1996 Gallery of Best Resumes for Two-Year Graduates," and she has been profiled in a variety of publications, including Carol Kleiman's syndicated column on careers and related issues.

Wittenstein prepares resumes for all professionals, from entry-level through senior management. Her scope of services includes cover letters, targeted employer mailings, Internet and scannable formats and Internet postings.

JANE B. WILSON

555 Main Street • Anytown, USA 00000   (000) XXX-XXXX

Objective:	Seeking employment as a **Special Education Teacher**

Profile:

- Energetic and people-oriented self-starter, with broad base of regular and special education teaching experience.
- Background includes exposure to inclusion, resource and self-contained classroom settings. Skilled in adapting curriculum to children's needs.

Education:

ANY STATE UNIVERSITY, Anytown, USA
Master of Arts, Special Education, May 1997
- Any State Type XX Certification, including: **Trainable Mentally Handicapped, Educable Mentally Handicapped, Learning Disabilities.**

UNIVERSITY OF ANYTOWN, Anytown, USA
Bachelor of Arts, Communication Studies, May 1994

Experience:

January 1997 -
March 1997

WESTOWN SCHOOL (District #XX), Anytown, USA
Student Teacher, Self-Contained, Cross Categorical Classroom (Grades 1-3)
- Collaborated with classroom teacher regarding all aspects of classroom activities and strategies. Taught all subjects to students.
- Created and implemented lesson plans (under direction of classroom teacher), including Life Skills units and incorporation of whole language.
- Responsible for developing individual behavior modification program, preparing IEPs, and attending both staff and team meetings.

August 1996 -
December 1996

PLEASANT FIELD SCHOOL (District #XX), Anytown, USA
Special Education - Educator's Associate (Grades 5 & 6)
- Provided classroom and resource room instruction to 15 inclusion students. Assisted in the following subjects: Spelling, Writing, Reading, Social Studies, Science and Mathematics.
- Administered Curriculum Based Measurements in Reading (CBM).
- Coached students in development of organizational skills.
- **Invited to return upon completion of student teaching.**

September 1995 -
June 1996

ANY PUBLIC SCHOOL SYSTEM (District #XX), Anytown, USA
Substitute Teacher (Grades K-8)
- Accepted assignments for six schools within this district.
- Classrooms included regular and special education, ESL, Gym, Music, Art and Library.

January 1995 -
June 1995

LEARN-A-LOT SCHOOL (District #XX), Anytown, USA
One-On-One Assistant
- Provided individual assistance to one five-year-old student with TMH within a cross-categorical, self-contained Kindergarten classroom.
- Assisted this student in all subject areas, as well as school activities, lunch and special programs. Provided support during seizures.

Affiliations: Council for Exceptional Children

References: Credential file available at Any State University.

This One's a Winner!

The Two-Pronged Approach to Successful Career Marketing

Peter sent this resume to 10 prospective employers and received seven offers for interviews. He accepted two and was hired by Lufthansa.

Why was he so successful?

"Peter's resume demonstrates our philosophy of 'marketing your skills and abilities' to employers," says Steven Provenzano, president of Advanced Resume Service, Inc., headquartered in Schaumburg, Ill.

"The Profile section is where you want to isolate and market your most relevant skills and abilities, no matter how they were acquired," the author explains. "The Employment and other sections then support these statements. It's a simple yet effective two-pronged approach that allows you to leverage the best you have to offer."

Provenzano also points out that the resume includes clear, high-impact, non-subjective language that Peter is comfortable with. Arrows break up the copy and add white space while drawing attention to accomplishments or interesting facts about work experience. All of these elements make the document easy on the eye.

To prepare this resume for use on Internet databases, Provenzano would save it in ASCII text, align the copy flush left and strip away all tabs and graphics, such as boldface type, underlining and arrows (which could be replaced by asterisks). He would then e-mail it directly to employers' databases, where it would be sorted by its keywords.

"Most of Peter's keywords are in the Profile section," he says, "and the computer would find them there."

Provenzano also advises including a desired geographic location (to eliminate calls from employers in areas where you wouldn't want to move) and an expiration date (three to six months from the posting date).

Steven Provenzano, CPRW
President, Advanced Resume Service, Inc.

Steven Provenzano, author of *Top Secret Resumes & Cover Letters*, is a Certified Professional Resume Writer (CPRW). His company, with offices in Schaumburg, Roselle and Streamwood, Ill., has written more than 9,000 resumes and provides full outplacement services.

In addition, Provenzano conducts resume writing and career marketing seminars for major companies and universities. He has written articles for such publications as the *National Business Employment Weekly* and *Chicago Tribune*, and has appeared several times on CNN and CNBC. Resume writing services are available worldwide through e-mail at ADVRESUMES@aol.com An article on effective resume writing can be found at Web site http://amsquare.com/america/advanced.html

---

PETER T. SOTTILE

5 Brookstone Court
Streamwood, IL 60107   630/555-2690

OBJECTIVE: *IMPORT / EXPORT OPERATIONS*
A position where safety, speed and reliability are used to satisfy the customer.

PROFILE:

▶   Experience in all aspects of air freight import and export, including full responsibility for customs documentation and aircraft loading/unloading.

▶   Effectively train, supervise and motivate teams in customer service, storage and documentation.

▶   Certified in the transport and acceptance of dangerous goods and Bonded by U.S. Customs.

▶   Proficient in the coordination/arrangement of freight and the cost-effective loading and unloading of cargo and passenger aircraft.

▶   Skilled in the use of USAS cargo application systems.

EMPLOYMENT: <u>Air France Cargo,</u> O'Hare Intnl. Airport, Chicago, IL and JFK Intnl. Airport, Jamaica, New York   12/81-Present

Lead Cargo Service Agent/Supervisor, O'Hare, IL   5/92-Present
Responsible for hiring, training and supervising a team of 40 employees in loading/unloading up to 200 tons of freight daily on freight/passenger aircraft and flatbed trucks.
Handle total configurations of freight for safe, economical transport.
Constantly track and investigate shipments and oversee tie-downs and palletizing at a 100,000 s.f. warehouse.
Communicate with customers on a daily basis regarding special handling and all shipping procedures.
Compile and update statistics on all import/export cargo with a computer used by the world's largest cargo airlines.

→   Work closely with customers to troubleshoot problems and locate items on flights and in warehouses worldwide.
→   Occasionally drive forklifts and other equipment to get the job done on time.
→   Assist in recruiting and interviewing new personnel; conduct regular staff performance reviews and act as employee representative.
→   Coordinate functions with U.S. Customs, freight brokers and service companies.

→   Gained an excellent knowledge of airline and cargo procedures.
→   Completed training in assertiveness, as well as warehouse and office skills.
→   Promoted to this position from:

Agent/Acting Supervisor, Chicago, IL   1/83-5/92
Worked closely with customers regarding shipment handling and procedures.
Negotiated freight contracts and trained/supervised several employees in all operations.

Cargo Handler/Warehouse, JFK, NY   Part-time, 12/81-1/83
Prepared cargo for transport and operated forklifts.
Assisted in warehouse setups, stocking and freight tracking.

ADDITIONAL EXPERIENCE

P.D. Prints, Streamwood, IL   Part-time, 10 hours/month 2/95-Present
Sales Representative
Involved in sales and order taking for specialty silk screen t-shirts, working primarily with employees from various airlines and cargo companies.

Sales Representative for one year at a retail store and **Cook** for two years with a catering company.
Also employed as **Passenger Agent** with a helicopter transportation company.

EDUCATION: Nassau Community College, Garden City, NY   1978-1980
Liberal Arts studies included computer science.

Wantagh High School, Wantagh, NY   Graduated 1978

CERTIFICATION: Certified in the transport and acceptance of dangerous goods and Bonded by U.S. Customs since 1983.

Power Resume Tip

Keep in mind that prospective employers will spend less than 30 seconds reviewing your resume. You must keep it clear, concise and focused on the information that will sell you best.

Making the Military to Management Connection

Translating Military Experience to Corporate Needs

"Creating winning resume presentations for military personnel can often be a daunting task," says Wendy Enelow, founder and president of The Advantage, Inc., an executive resume and career marketing firm.

"It's critical that the resume present the military experience in a manner that 'connects' it with the skills, qualifications and experience level required for a position in 'Corporate America.'"

To meet this challenge, Enelow used a modified format that integrates the best of both chronological and functional resume styles. She began with a paragraph-style Career Profile to briefly highlight overall qualifications (and not start the resume with U.S. Army!). Within the Professional Experience section:

- The introductory paragraph and list of honors quickly demonstrates this individual's successful career performance and advancement.

- The functional category listings (e.g., Operations Management, Human Resources, Budgeting, Safety, Technology, Flight Operations, Project Leadership, Communications) visually highlight each core competency, translating them from "military lingo" into "corporate lingo."

- The achievements under each category clearly demonstrate the scope of responsibility and significant achievements.

The resume is quick to read, easy to understand and directly applicable to a broad range of general management positions. Most significant, it is not tied to any particular industry, allowing this candidate the flexibility to conduct a broad and cross-industry job search.

Wendy S. Enelow, CPRW
Founder and President, The Advantage, Inc.

Wendy S. Enelow is a nationally recognized expert in the field of executive job search. Her recent publication, *100 Winning Resumes for $100,000+ Jobs,* (Impact Publications, 1997) has received widespread acclaim and she is currently completing the upcoming *201 Winning Cover Letters for $100,000+ Jobs* (Impact Publications, 1997).

Enelow's resumes have been reprinted in *Top 100 Resumes* and *Gallery of Best Resumes.* She has recently been featured in *Your Outplacement Handbook* and *Fortune* magazine's *Keep Your Job* videotape. Her articles have appeared in *National Business Employment Weekly,* Joyce Lain Kennedy's nationally syndicated job-search column, *Northeast PA Employment Weekly* and in numerous Internet sites (see http://www.inmind.com/advantage).

Enelow is a Certified Professional Resume Writer (CPRW) and served a two-year term on the executive board of the Professional Association of Resume Writers.

STEPHEN P. O'CALLAHAN

PACCOM HEADQUARTERS
Unit 987314 Box 1000
APO, AE 19148
Home: 011-82-999-555-5678
Office: 011-82-999-333-1234

CAREER PROFILE

Distinguished management career leading the planning, staffing, budgeting, technology and operations of organizations throughout the U.S. and abroad. Expert in cross-functional team building and leadership, multi-cultural communications, change management, organization development and quality/performance improvement. Travelled, lived and/or worked in more than 30 countries worldwide.

PROFESSIONAL EXPERIENCE:

UNITED STATES ARMY   1974 to Present

Branch Chief / Commanding Officer / Executive Officer
Operations Officer / Logistics Officer / Safety Director

Fast-track career promotion through a series of increasingly responsible management positions leading large-scale operations worldwide. Currently holds the rank of Lieutenant Colonel. Honored with numerous commendations and awards for outstanding leadership, general management and field operations:

- Meritorious Service Medals (2)
- Meritorious Unit Commendation
- Army Unit Commendation
- Air Medal
- Joint Service Commendation Medal
- Presidential Service Badge
- Humanitarian Service Medal
- Combat Action Ribbon

Operations Management

- Twenty years' management experience in the strategic planning, staffing, budgeting, resource allocation and leadership of administrative, field, flight, maintenance, equipment, technology, training and logistics operations worldwide. Skilled policy-maker.
- Direct and decisive leadership qualifications with particular strengths in planning, performance improvement, quality improvement and productivity gain.
- Experienced in the start-up and leadership of new operations and organizations.

Human Resource Affairs & Team Leadership

- Led teams of up to 500 personnel with full responsibility for work assignments, scheduling, performance review, disciplinary action and long-term career planning/development/promotion.
- Expert qualifications in evaluating personnel needs and developing responsive training programs.
- Early career experience managing the audit and examination of personnel records to ensure regulatory compliance.

Budgeting & Financial Management

- Administered up to $50 million in annual budgets to support operations worldwide.
- Expert in evaluating organizational funding requirements, preparing/leading formal budget presentations, allocating the distribution of funds, and managing complex financial analysis and reporting functions.

Safety Management

- Extensive qualifications in the planning, development and leadership of occupational, workplace, transportation and aviation safety programs supporting operations throughout the U.S. and abroad.
- Equally extensive qualifications in safety training program design and instruction.

Technology Management

- Spearheaded the operational test, analysis and review of advanced navigational, telecommunications and operating support systems to evaluate performance and reliability.
- PC skills in word processing, database and spreadsheet applications.

Flight Operations

- Planned, staffed, budgeted and directed flight transportation operations worldwide.
- Directed flight planning and scheduling, aircraft operations, aircraft maintenance, aviator training and flight instructor training programs.
- Designated Flight Officer with over 6100 hours of total flight time with no incidents.
- Four-year tenure ás Presidential Command Pilot.

Project Coordination & Leadership

- Planned and directed cooperative operations between the U.S., France, Germany and United Kingdom through direct leadership of multinational teams.
- Led joint efforts on behalf of the U.S. Government, U.S. embassies, Pentagon and State Department to facilitate emergency relief, assistance and humanitarian programs.

Communications

- Strong communications, public speaking and senior-level presentation experience.

EDUCATION:

MA (International Relations), New York University, 1985
BA (History), University of Michigan, 1974

Graduate of numerous management and leadership training programs including the prestigious Army Command & Staff College.

References Provided Upon Request

Power Resume Tip

When you summarize your responsibilities, use action words, such as "directed," "created," "implemented," etc., and avoid repeating the same words.

Show That You Have What It Takes

Use Projects to Reveal Accomplishments, Skills

Certain professionals (such as architects, engineers, interior designers, construction managers, senior-level computer programmers or consultants of any kind) will find that including a subheading for major projects may strengthen their ability to compete for interviews, advises Joanne Kowlowitz, the director of The Advantage of Maryland in Catonsville, Md.

"Often the candidate's professional qualifications and the level of his or her abilities are best 'sold' by highlighting the scope of the projects they've worked on," she says. "For example, the individual who was responsible for a $110 million steel construction project would be required to have a certain degree of technical, management and decision-making skills to accomplish a task of that magnitude."

A prospective employer who gives only a quick read to the scores of resumes on his desk need only to glance at the Project Highlights section to be convinced that this candidate has what it takes.

"By using this resume style, you not only minimize lengthy and often repetitious job descriptions, but also you boost your competitive edge by showing your career accomplishments in an interesting and easy-to-read fashion," Kowlowitz concludes.

Joanne Kowlowitz
Director, The Advantage of Maryland

The Advantage has set the standard for professional resume preparation in the Baltimore area for more than a decade. Mentored by Wendy S. Enelow, recognized nationwide as an expert in executive job search, Joanne Kowlowitz has established her own reputation as a savvy job search consultant and skilled writer.

Kowlowitz specializes in resume writing for career change, executive networking and federal employment for all professional levels and industry types. She also writes for marketing and corporation communication projects and has been featured in various local and regional publications.

PHILLIP S. KRAEMER

8005 Nottingham Way
Baltimore, Maryland 21209
410-555-5665

CAREER PROFILE

PROJECT MANAGER / DESIGN & ENGINEERING PROFESSIONAL

Senior-level experience in the strategic planning and profitable management of multimillion dollar engineering and construction projects. Specialize in advanced civil engineering and site development with the proven ability to create solutions to diverse, and often complex functional, environmental and aesthetic challenges. Consistently successful in completing projects under budget and well within time lines.

Expert team builder and organizational leader with the ability to generate cooperation among all levels of personnel. Focused, confident and decisive professional with a visionary and consistent management style. Unblemished reputation for professional ethics and personal integrity.

PROFESSIONAL EXPERIENCE

Capital Project Manager   1991 to Present
BRIDGEGAP, LTD., Silver Spring, Maryland

Highly-visible Project Manager and Lead Civil Engineer position responsible for the strategic planning and management of large-scale engineering and construction projects. Conduct field site inspections of projects (prospective, new, ongoing and completed) with a primary focus on analyzing usage, cost containment, quality assurance and regulatory compliance factors. Recruit, train and supervise a staff of 14 engineers and field inspectors.

Directly responsible for the development and implementation of design solutions and job-site problem resolution. Lead weekly progress meetings with architects, engineers and trade contractors, and conduct frequent briefings with top-level management. Interface extensively with owners, banking executives, subcontractors, suppliers, and federal/state/local inspection and regulatory officials.

Project Highlights:

- $120 million road and overpass construction project - New Jersey State Highway Administration.
- Sampson County Marina, Sampson County, Connecticut - $44 million new construction project including marina facility; 2 miles of mountain access road; 2-lane boat ramp; and 200-space parking area.
- Mount Blanc Park, Centre City, Pennsylvania - $56 million new construction including water, sewer and electrical connections for the main facility and seven outbuildings; 1.5 mile access road; and 45 camping pads.

Director of Engineering   1989 to 1991
SYLVESTER & SYLVESTER, West Martin, Virginia

Responsible technical operations and business management functions for a well-established civil engineering firm. Generated new business, developed proposals, conducted feasibility analyses, negotiated contracts and oversaw daily business operations. Administered a $7.5 million operating budget and hired, supervised and evaluated the work performance of a staff of 23.

Project Highlights:

- $16.2 million, 54-lot single family subdivision (completed this project $5.2 million under budget and 6 weeks ahead of schedule).
- $4 million construction project for 200,000 sq. ft. office and retail space.
- $3.6 million, 20-lot single family subdivision.

PROFESSIONAL EXPERIENCE (Continued)

Project Manager   1987 to 1989
RAISTON, KULSKI & FITCH, West Mount, Virginia

Directly responsible for design, engineering, surveying, project scheduling, proposal preparation and presentation, site supervision and problem resolution. Represented clients in negotiations with county, city, state and regulatory compliance officials. Promoted within one year from Engineer to Project Manager.

Project Highlights:

- $5.5 million construction project for 14-acre residential development.
- $30 million, 300-unit luxury condominium construction project.

EDUCATION

M.S., Environmental Engineering, 1993
THE GEORGE WASHINGTON UNIVERSITY, Washington, D.C.

B.S., Civil Engineering, 1989
UNIVERSITY OF MARYLAND, College Park, Maryland

PROFESSIONAL AFFILIATIONS

Board of Directors, District of Columbia Association of Civil Engineers
Member, American Association of Civil Engineers
Member, American Association of Design Engineers
Selection Committee, Senior Engineering Professionals and Project Managers, Bridgegap, Ltd.

AWARD

First Place, Engineering Design Competition, American Association of Design Engineers, 1993

References and Portfolio Provided Upon Request
Willing to Travel or Relocate

Power Resume Tip

You may want to mention any unique educational experience you've had, such as spending a year as a foreign exchange student, or as an intern. Even if these experiences aren't directly linked to your career goal, they indicate that you are a person who is open to new opportunities and challenges.

Shedding the "Old" Image

Addressing Age and Time Gaps in Your Resume

Lynn Wood is a dynamic, versatile and personable health care professional who had been out of the job force for some time to care for her terminally ill father. Using a combination format to emphasize accomplishments and quantifiable results while downplaying the work history, Nancy Karvonen, president and owner of A Better Word & Resume, was able to label that valuable nonpaid experience as a *resource consultant* to fill the time gap.

"Lynn's 20 years' traffic supervisor experience was shown as *prior experience* to avoid the 'older worker' image, yet show her supervisory capabilities," explains Karvonen, a Certified Professional Resume Writer (CPRW). "Discriminate use of bold typeface highlights her accomplishments. In addition, her extensive community involvement effectively positioned her as a strong resource contact."

Lynn had a solid background in her field. Although she wanted to remain in her remote northern California area, this goal-oriented job seeker was willing to relocate to any geographical or related area to obtain a position. As a result, her resume was rearranged to fit several different job objectives.

Karvonen comments that Lynn did all the right things in her thorough job search, including a professionally prepared resume and cover letter, follow-up thank you letters, video interview training and Internet posting.

"Her diligent marketing campaign efforts paid off in securing her dream job as an executive with a progressive local health care facility," adds Karvonen. "She loves her position, especially when people stop to tell her they're glad she's working there because she does such a good job."

Nancy Karvonen, CPRW
President, A Better Word & Resume

Nancy Karvonen, a Certified Professional Resume Writer and member of the Professional Association of Resume Writers, is president and owner of A Better Word & Resume in Willits, Calif. She has a comprehensive career background in technical, secretarial, medical and nontraditional fields, which she finds beneficial in working with clients from blue collar to executive levels. As a job-search consultant, she frequently presents resume-writing and job-search seminars to colleges and the community. Karvonen also mentors new resume writers. Her resumes have been featured in *101 Best Resumes* and *Resume Pro Newsletter*.

Lynn Wood

1021 Lake Mendocino Drive • Ukiah, California 95482 • (707) 462-4142

OBJECTIVE   A position as Director/Counselor/Educator/Case Manager/Coordinator

PROFILE
- More than 15 years experience as professional manager.
- Ability to direct complex projects from concept to fully operational status.
- Goal-oriented individual with strong leadership capabilities.
- Organized, highly motivated, and detail directed problem solver.
- Proven ability to work in unison with staff, volunteers and Board of Directors.

EDUCATION   M.A., Gerontology, Sonoma State University
B.A., Psychology and Gerontology, Cum Laude, Sonoma State University

RELEVANT EXPERIENCE AND ACCOMPLISHMENTS

PROGRAM COORDINATION
- Successfully established new Adult Day Health Care Program.
- Balanced **$1.5 million budget**, resulting in impressive 15 percent profit margin.
- Managed $650,000 senior center building project.
- **Wrote grants, secured funding** and established Peer Counseling Program for seniors.
- Reorganized In-Home Program, **turning annual $11,000 loss to $40,000** profit.
- Created Thrift/Gift/Craft Shop producing annual net profit of $36,000.
- Designed service development plans and conducted operation assessments.
- Counseled students on defining career and work related goals and objectives.
- Formulated, wrote, and implemented new employee orientation manuals.

MANAGEMENT/SUPERVISION
- Directed recruitment and retention of supervisors and staff of 42 employees.
- Trained, supervised and evaluated staff, coached improvement management skills.
  - Resulted in multilateral staff achievement of work objectives.
- Managed and developed over 200 volunteers into goal-oriented, cohesive group.
- Successfully refined and **implemented new projects**.

EMPLOYMENT HISTORY

1994-present   **Resource Consultant** • Health Care Resource Services, Ukiah
Provide private professional case management service for dependent adults.

1989-1994   **Executive Director** • Ukiah Senior Center, Ukiah
Oversaw operations of daily senior programs for 300 clients at 25,000 sq. ft. facility. Directed transportation, adult day health care, home delivered meals, nutrition, outreach, Alzheimer's, **in-home care**, and peer counseling.

1988-1989   **Teaching Assistant** • Gerontology Program, Sonoma State University
Student-taught death and dying class and inter-generational relations.

1985-1988   **Counselor in Education** • Mendocino Community College, Ukiah
Counseled students on securing OJT college credits for Work Experience Program.

Prior Experience   **Traffic Supervisor** • Pacific Telephone Company, Ukiah
Trained and supervised traffic control operators and wrote new employee manuals.

COMMUNITY INVOLVEMENT
Ukiah Valley Medical Center, Board Of Directors and Strategic Planning Committee
Leadership Mendocino Steering Committee, Secretary
Greater Ukiah Chamber of Commerce, President, Board of Directors
Soroptomist of Yokayo Sunrise, Member

HONORS AND AWARDS
Distinguished Human Services Recipient • *Woman of Achievement* • *Solving the Generation Gap*

Every Resume Tells a Story

Letting the Real You Shine Through

Its highly readable and effective job descriptions attracted Murray B. Parker to this resume. Parker is founder and president of The Borton Wallace Company, a retained search consultancy in the pulp and paper industry based in Asheville, N.C. For instance, this candidate, James Rogers, has clearly laid out his career in chronological order, listing each position, describing the nature and scope of environment and *briefly* explaining his accountabilities.

This establishes a frame of reference for the most important part of his resume, the Key Accomplishments. Here, James is able to clearly spell out his impact on the business. Not his activities, but his results. What he accomplished is stated in easy-to-understand specific terms such as dollars saved annually or percentage of improvement. These are the claims that will make a prospective employer sit up and take notice.

Note, too, that despite all of the description, the candidate designed the resume with a terrific amount of white space, making it highly readable and scannable.

"This resume tells the candidate's story most effectively, clearly and in the shortest space possible," says Parker. "After all, with a resume it's important to be clear and easy to read, yet answer all the key questions an employer might have."

Murray B. Parker
Founder and President, The Borton Wallace Company

Murray B. Parker is a charter member and director of the National Association of Executive Recruiters and a member of the Technical Association of Pulp & Paper Industry. He generated two patents and several million pounds-per-year products while at DuPont, then pursued a petroleum products new venture before embarking on his professional recruiting career.

Founded in 1978, The Borton Wallace Company is a retained search consultancy focused on technical and operations functions within the pulp and paper and supplier industries.

JAMES ROGERS

55 Silver Court   Home: (301) 555-7275
Mallard, MD 21178   Office: (301) 555-6345

OBJECTIVE: Challenging operations management position at the corporate, division, or business unit level where broad management skills in operations management can be fully utilized.

PROFESSIONAL HIGHLIGHTS:

1989   SOFT SPRITZ CORPORATION, COLLEGE PARK, MD
to
Present   Group Plant Manager, Silver Springs, MD (10/89 to Present)
Report to Division Operations Manager of this $5 billion, Fortune 200, beverage and fast foods company. Full P&L responsibility for management of $50 million budget, 15 million unit, 140 employee soft drink bottling operation. Functional accountabilities include production operations, plant engineering, warehousing, distribution, and quality control.

Key Accomplishments:

- Directed successful $2 million redesign/rebuild of manufacturing facility (annual savings $700 thousand).

- Reduced workforce by 28% through reconfiguration of bottling line and warehouse methods improvement (annual savings $400 thousand).

- Created task force that reduced product "shrinkage" by 85% (annual savings $425 thousand).

- Initiated "driver assist" program reducing warehouse loading crew by 30% and overtime hours by 8 thousand per year (annual savings $220 thousand).

Acquisitions/Special Projects Manager (1/89-10/89)
College Park, MD
Reported to Vice President of Operations.
Responsible for directing the smooth transition of 3 newly acquired franchise bottling plants into the Soft Spritz corporate plant network environment. Directed activities of 3 plant managers in installation of administrative systems that resulted in significantly improved operating results.

Key Accomplishments:

- Led corporate headquarters staff team in the development of a strategic model to guide all future business expansion and site selection.

- Directed "sourcing needs" study of Western Region resulting in shutdown of bottling facility ($800 thousand annual savings).

- Directed warehouse consolidation project in Western Region, consolidating 3 high cost warehouses into 1 new strategically located facility ($800 thousand annual savings).

- Initiated labor control reports allowing management to eliminate wasted manpower (annual savings $200 thousand).

1975
to
1989

FAMOUS BEVERAGE COMPANY, PITTSBURGH, PA
Plant Manager, Pittsburgh, PA (1985-1989)
Reported to Division Operations Manager. Directed staff of 5 with full P&L responsibility for operation of 2 bottling plants (190 employees, 15 million units, $45 million budget). Functional accountability for production, maintenance, warehousing, and quality.

Key Accomplishments:

- Served on Board of Directors of Wilson Packaging Cooperative (1981-1989) with significant improvement to operating results (annual savings $1.5 million).

- Reduced overall operating costs by 31% while increasing production volume by 19%.

- Directed successful installation of $5 million bottling equipment resulting in 25% reduction in headcount (annual savings $1.1 million).

Plant Manager, Beaver, PA (1980-1985)
Reported to Division Operations Manager. Full P&L responsibility for 160 employee, $40 million, 9 million unit soft drink bottling operation.

Plant Manager III, Detroit, MI (1979-1980)
Reported to Division Operations Manager with P&L responsibility for 100 employee, 4 million unit bottling operation (annual budget $20 million).

Production Manager, Detroit, MI (1978-1979)

Ass't Production Manager, Detroit, MI (1975-1978)

EDUCATION: B.S., Engineering, University of Michigan
Major: Mechanical Engineering

REFERENCES: Excellent references available upon request.

Power Resume Tip

Make sure your resume is neat, clean and easy to read. Type and white space should be arranged so that the reader's eye is drawn quickly from beginning to end.

Making Two Pages into One

When Two Pages are Too Many

Many people have skills, experience and achievements which justify a two-page resume. But Erin Flanagan, a client of Kathleen Brogan's, refused the first draft of a two-page version and insisted on a one-page resume.

They were able to accomplish the task by beginning with an overall summary of skills and drastically condensing the content of each section.

"We followed Erin's key responsibilities with major achievements and quantified results whenever possible, such as in sales increases and cost savings," says Brogan, whose business is located in Minneapolis, Minn.

Should you decide on a similar format, Brogan advises taking time to carefully assess your range of skills, primary responsibilities and accomplishments. Include only the most important ones. For example, focus on major projects, the role(s) you played and what outcome(s) resulted. By incorporating bullets, you will gain space and enhance your resume's readability.

"Be sure you demonstrate your qualifications," stresses Brogan, "including leadership, initiative, creativity, problem-solving skills, and your ability to learn and implement new information. Be truthful and honest. Chances are you'll be proud of the resume you create."

Kathleen Brogan
Brogan Communications

Kathleen Brogan has been writing resumes, business/personal communications and humorous tributes since 1984. Prior to her writing career, she worked for eight years as a C.P.A. Brogan shares with her customers employment tips, interview strategies, advice and a few great one-liners.

ERIN A. FLANAGAN

317 Shamrock Lane
Emerald City, MN 55555
(612) 123-4567

KEY STRENGTHS

- ◆ Strategic Planning
- ◆ Innovation and Creativity
- ◆ Initiative and Problem Solving
- ◆ Project Management
- ◆ Communication and Interpersonal Skills
- ◆ International Experience

EMPLOYMENT HISTORY

FOOD WORLD, Minneapolis, MN   11/95-Present
Senior Promotions Planner

Manage the strategic development/execution of promotional plans for multiple cereal brands.
Utilize a diverse range of vehicles from couponing and sampling to event marketing with retailers.
Responsible for a combined budget of $56 million.

- Developed promotional plan for company's second largest new product introduction.
- Spearheaded repositioning of Clusters cereal which increased sales 21%.
- Initiated several breakthrough couponing and sampling plans; achieved savings of $2.5mm.
- Managed national and regional marketing events generating promotional volume of 15$^+$%.

FOUR STAR PROMOTIONS, Minneapolis, MN   7/94-11/95
New Business Development

Created and led Sales Promotion unit identifying and securing new business opportunities.
Served as Account Director for new clients managing all activity from strategic promotion planning
   to program execution.

- Secured 7 new clients and related revenue of $2mm.
- Developed all sales materials and product literature.

CEREALS, INC., Seattle, WA   10/89-3/94
Senior Promotions Manager, 4/92-3/94
Brand Manager, 7/91-3/92
Assistant Brand Manager, 10/89-7/91

Created Promotions Department executing 40 premium and 5 integrated marketing events annually.
Developed and implemented promotional plans for all 14 company products.

- Received 2 ISP (Promotions Industry) Awards.
- Established standards for premiums, product quality, product safety
  and supplier requirements.

Brand Manager of Shreddies franchise responsible for strategic development and execution
of marketing plans.

- Generated franchise growth of 11%.
- Developed first ever advertising campaign for Frosted Shreddies increasing penetration
  by 13% and brand awareness by 28%.

EDUCATION

UNIVERSITY OF CHICAGO, Chicago, IL   1987
Bachelor of Science degree in Economics

BONSAI COMPANY, Tokyo, Japan   1987
Marketing Internship

A Techie Resume That Makes Sense

Don't Baffle Them With Jargon

"An individual with a technical background might find it challenging to present his or her skills in a clear and concise manner," says Ann Wallace of Career Development Services.

While the inclusion of some jargon is good because it convinces the reviewer that you are intimate with the industry or specialty, you must remember that your resume might first be screened by nontechnical employees.

"In this resume, Thomas Romano does an excellent job describing his background, accomplishments and expertise to potential employers," says Wallace. "More specifically, this combination format resume is attractive, free of irrelevant data and provides just enough information to provoke the reader's interest. Romano effectively presents his accomplishments through bulleted, short and punchy sentences."

The action words he has chosen, such as "developed," "directed" and "consulted" immediately emphasize his strengths.

"In addition, he sums up his technical qualifications succinctly for those interested in this sort of information. But other than in the Technical Summary, Romano uses no other technical jargon."

Ann Wallace
Career Development Services

Career Development Services, located in Rochester, N.Y., is a nonprofit corporation providing comprehensive career planning services to individuals and organizations locally and nationally. The corporation is committed to identifying and addressing work force change issues through a variety of initiatives. These include assisting clients with formulating and implementing career and/or educational goals; consulting with employers to improve the quality of work life; and providing comprehensive resources, research and information on careers and related issues.

THOMAS A. ROMANO
35 Main Street
Syracuse, New York 13210
315-555-4444

SUMMARY OF QUALIFICATIONS

Twenty years of progressive Management Information Systems experience in financial, human resources, sales marketing and manufacturing systems. Experienced manager with strengths in systems development and implementation for both large and small organizations.

- Creatively resolved business systems issues.
- Organized and motivated project team members.
- Designed and implemented M.I.S. systems resulting in cost savings and improved departmental efficiencies.
- Successfully and consistently developed M.I.S. systems on time and within budget.

TECHNICAL SUMMARY

• DOS/VSE	• VM	• CA/SORT	• CA/DYNMT
• CICS	• COBOL	• CA/GL	• MSA/FIXED
• VSAM	• CMS	• CA/AP	ASSETS
• MSA/AR	• PC-S	• CA/RAPS	

MANAGEMENT

- Managed the consolidation of financial and human resource systems of two major divisions.
- Developed, designed and implemented 18 M.I.S. systems.
- Directed a staff of six programmers and systems analysts.
- Conducted feasibility and equipment analysis studies for corporate needs.
- Consulted in the installation of MSA and COMPUTER ASSOCIATES software packages.
- Developed new M.I.S. standards and procedures for the systems and operational areas.
- Planned and managed project implementation schedules.
- Managed a wide range of applications such as: payroll, sales, costing, budgeting, distribution, invoicing, accounts payable and receivable, order entry and inventory.

TRAINING

- Developed, implemented and conducted formal training programs and presentations for all levels of management.
- Conducted pre- and post-implementation training on installed packages.
- Conducted orientation and training sessions for new programming staff.
- Organized and presented professional seminars.

COMMUNICATIONS

- Interacted and coordinated with other corporate divisions and departments in the planning, development and implementation of new M.I.S. systems.
- Analyzed and selected various vendor packages.
- Developed written proposals to support new systems and programs.

EMPLOYMENT

ABC Company, Project Manager	1988-present
XYZ Company, Senior Systems Analyst	1980-1988
XOX Products, Inc., Operations Manager/Programmer	1978-1980

EDUCATION

Electronic Computer Programming Institute
Graduated with High Honors, 1986

Northern Georgia University
B.S., Business

PROFESSIONAL/COMMUNITY AFFILIATIONS

- Past president and director of the Syracuse Lions Club.
- Past president and director of the ABC Management Club.
- Past president of the Central New York Chapter of the Association of Systems Management.
- Membership committee member of the Syracuse Chapter of the Association of Systems Management.

Power Resume Tip

Spotlight your most important sales points. Your most impressive and relevant qualifications should be highlighted with boldface type or other design elements, so they will be immediately apparent to someone scanning your resume.

When a Functional Resume Makes Sense

For a Candidate Who Didn't Follow a Traditional Path

"A functional resume such as Ellen Azevedo's is particularly effective for candidates whose important work skills were acquired outside the usual full-time employment environment," says Louis Persico. He is founder and president of Career Management Consultants, Inc.

"Although many experts advise against using a functional resume format, it is a useful tool for people making career changes or for those who need to highlight skills and achievements they've developed away from work."

Persico points out that Azevedo's resume was key in her securing a position as a publications editor for a leading trade association although she hadn't worked full-time for 16 years. "She had developed most of the skills she needed for the position through volunteer work, irregular freelance assignments and part-time work. The functional format was particularly helpful during her networking interviews because the listing of her capability areas stood out visually and could be understood at a glance."

Persico explains, "All resumes are sales documents. They are brochures designed to demonstrate value to the potential buyer (employer). In deciding what information to include, job seekers should ask if the information demonstrates experience, skills, knowledge or personality traits that would have value to a potential employer.

"The bottom-line criterion for inclusion of information revolves around value and includes performance. Thus, the functional resume should list not only what the candidate has done, but how well he or she has done it."

Although Azevedo's resume demonstrates almost nothing in the way of traditional job experience, it does demonstrate skills that an employer looking for a skilled communicator would desire.

Louis Persico
Founder, President, Career Management Consultants, Inc.

Louis Persico is founder and president of Career Management Consultants, Inc., a firm providing corporate-sponsored outplacement and individual career transition services. As the oldest firm of its kind in Harrisburg, Pa., CMC offers a full range of individual and group outplacement programs, customized to meet the needs of clients and sponsoring companies.

An important service of CMC is the quarterly, *Career Outplacement Newsletter*, published by Persico and edited by Kate Duttro, D.Ed., freelance writer on business, career and cross-cultural topics. Several articles that originally appeared in the newsletter have been reprinted for other publications, including *The Wall Street Journal's National Business Employment Weekly*.

Persico is a Certified Career Management Fellow of the International Board for Career Management Certification.

ELLEN AZEVEDO

40 Blue Ridge Road
Lancaster, PA 17601
(717) 555-1111

OBJECTIVE: A program coordinator or public relations position requiring creativity with refined oral/written communicating, organizing and instructing skills.

QUALIFICATIONS: Solid experience in initiating, implementing and promoting agency programs. Successful free-lance writing experience.

CAPABILITY AREAS: <u>SPECIFIC RELATED ACCOMPLISHMENTS</u>

PUBLIC RELATIONS: Researched functions, needs and goals of 4 social service agencies. Wrote/edited newsletters and brochures. Publications cited by boards and staffs for contributions to public image and fund raising.

COMMUNICATING: Successfully researched and wrote 40 human interest articles published in 9 major regional and national publications including <u>Jamestown Enquirer</u> (circ. 323,000) and <u>Working Parent</u> (circ. 220,000).

Co-authored 175-page novel praised by Penguin Publishing Co. executive editor for "good writing and perceptive characterization."

ORGANIZING: Perceived need for Episcopal parish. Recruited members, procured meeting place and convened meetings. Served as elected lay leader for 3 years, overseeing all committees. By end of term, congregation had purchased and renovated a church building and hired a pastor.

Started church-based Central America committee. Organized and presented recruitment programs, obtained sponsorship and acted as liaison with other groups. Coordinated letter writing campaigns and initiated Guatemalan sister parish relationship. Committee's vibrancy/commitment recognized in annual parish report.

INSTRUCTING: Designed and conducted college level writing course for an industrial setting. Secured supplemental materials and fashioned course around <u>Grapes of Wrath</u>. Received high student evaluations for creativity and interest.

Initiated and taught high school creative writing course and published first literary magazine. Commended by department head for organization and teaching ability.

EXPERIENCE: Free-lance Writer, 1984 - Present.

Real Estate Broker, Jonesville, Iowa, 1981 - 1983.

Adjunct Writing Instructor, Jonesville University, Jonesville, Iowa, 1976 - 1979.

English Teacher, 1969 - 1976.

OTHER EXPERIENCE: Consultant, Brochure Development, Family Children's Center, Lancaster, PA, 1988.

Consultant, Editorial and Public Relations, Sunshine Youth Home, Westville, Idaho, 1987.

EDUCATION: M.A.T., Education (major field, English)
Temple University, Philadelphia, PA, 1974

B.S. Education
Temple University, Philadelphia, PA, 1969
GPA: 3.3

ADDITIONAL SKILLS: Word Processing

Power Resume Tip

If your resume is two pages long, add the word "continued" at the bottom of the first page, and put your name and the words "page 2" at the top of the second page just in case pages become separated once your resume is in the hands of your prospective employer.

A Blue Collar Worker with a Red Flag

Showcasing a Job Hopper with a Varied Background

Author and outplacement specialist Anne Follis offers this resume of a blue collar worker with a recent history of job hopping.

"Like so many people these days, Monty has a varied background," she explains. "He was a custodian for a number of years, and during that time he gained supervisory experience. Recently, he decided to try truck driving. He's moved through several driving positions in a short time, which isn't at all uncommon in his field."

So how do you avoid appearing to be a job hopper, a red flag that Follis says is sure to bump your resume out of the running for many employers?

She addresses the issue by highlighting Monty's skills, including driving, heavy equipment operation, personnel supervision and customer service, in a Profile section at the top of the page. She points out that this format allows him to use this resume for any number of positions. Follis then details each position in the Experience section and groups his truck driving jobs to de-emphasize his jumping around.

"Although he did jump around as a driver, Monty's resume shows a history of stability in his other jobs," she adds. "It also shows he has stayed with truck driving, even though he's changed companies."

Anne Follis, CPRW
Owner/Manager, CareerPro

Anne Follis is a freelance writer and author of two books, including *Power Pack Your Job Search!* She also is an outplacement specialist, a Certified Professional Resume Writer (CPRW) and the owner and manager of CareerPro in Peoria, Ill.

Follis prepares original resumes and business materials for corporate and individual clients at all levels, conducts outplacement seminars and counsels on career decisions. She brings a background of author, educator, lecturer and public relations administrator to her job of helping others in their quest for employment. She can be reached at her e-mail address: alive90@aol.com

MONTY FREEDMAN

1234 N. Emerson • Peoria, IL 61111
Telephone: (309) 123-4567

PROFILE
- ► CDL driver's license with hazardous materials endorsement, over the road experience, and an excellent driving record.
- ► Able to operate a variety of heavy equipment including loggers, roll offs, and dump trucks.
- ► Background in personnel supervision, project management, facilities maintenance, and customer service.
- ► Personable and outgoing; excellent customer relations skills; work well under pressure; conscientious and willing to learn.

EXPERIENCE

Driver

HAYES TRANSPORT - East Peoria, IL	6/96 to Present
JENSEN, INC. - Peoria, IL	2/96 to 6/96
GILLES NATIONAL - Green Bay, WI	10/95 to 1/96

Transport a variety of materials and communicate with commercial clients, using judgment in resolving problems. Work without supervision; consistently meet deadlines.

Supervisor   9/90 to 9/95
HARDESTY MAINTENANCE OF ILLINOIS - Peoria, IL

Supervised 15+ employees and up to 50 for special projects for this outside contractor to Caterpillar. Directed various projects ranging from janitorial to first step maintenance. Operated a variety of machinery including power sweepers and oil pumps. Performed maintenance on cooling systems as needed. Maintained inventory of supplies. Began as general worker; **promoted** to lead position within six months; **promoted** to supervisor one year later.

Custodian   6/89 to 10/95
KNOX COLLEGE - Galesburg, IL

Cleaned equipment and facilities and trained workers.

EDUCATION

Completed Over-the-Road Training
STEVENSON TRAINING CENTER

Studies included hazardous materials, air brakes, accident prevention, right-to-know, skid pads, and OSHA regulations.

Training on floor care equipment.

REFERENCES AVAILABLE ON REQUEST

Spare the Details...Please

Resume Advice for Older Job Applicants

When 64-year-old John Smith met Peggy Hendershot, his resume was three pages long and crammed with highly detailed, technical information. As you can see, Hendershot, director of Career Planning Services at Career Vision, helped Smith fashion a highly readable two-page document.

"The resume is not an autobiography, but a teaser to encourage a personal contact and interview," says Hendershot. "In most cases, the job seeker is unable to tailor each resume for a specific position. Therefore, the identification of transferable skills becomes critical. In many cases, similar skills are used in various positions. It is helpful to stress different abilities, rather than emphasize similar activities repeatedly."

Smith's resume demonstrates technical and supervisory skills, individual and group problem-solving capabilities and leadership skill in an electronic research and development environment. It does this while providing the reader plenty of "breathing room" with white space, lines between bulleted items and a wide left margin.

"Smith's resume is a flexible tool for his job search effort," says Hendershot. "In the Professional Summary, the job seeker has identified the type of responsibilities for which he is best suited and supports that with specific statements in the body of the resume that also demonstrate the strengths Smith claimed to have."

Peggy Hendershot
Director of Career Planning Services, Career Vision

Peggy Hendershot is the director of career planning services for Career Vision. The firm, with offices in the Chicago area, offers a distinctive approach to career planning for individuals and organizations. Counselors help individuals with an improved self-understanding through a comprehensive assessment process that integrates aptitude, interests, personality, values and skills. This multiple assessment is invaluable in the identification of appropriate career paths and/or the selection of continuing education programs.

ELLIOT SHERWOOD
9876 Main Street
Small Town, IL 35455

*PROFESSIONAL
SUMMARY*

Electronics Engineer with more than 20 years of experience in research and development. Background in telecommunications, fire alarms and consumer electronics. Skilled at problem identification and resolution. Seven patents.

*WORK
EXPERIENCE*

Major Corporation, International   **1989—1997**
Serious, Illinois
Technical Team Leader

- Engineering/Production liaison for Digital Loop Carrier, "DLC". Successfully identified and solved design related production problems.
- Wrote requirements documents and test plans for Digital Loop Carrier $24 million system).
- Led hardware design of an Automated Test System which resulted in a 50% saving of time test.
- Simplified test procedures, cutting three hours from the final test of each DLC system.

Engineering Supervisor

- Supervised design of Channel Bank, both for voice and data. Accounted for $2 million annual sales.
- Coordinated the design of T-carrier synchronization system, from start to production. One million dollars annual sales.
- Led the complete design of division's first microprocessor controlled system and first U.L. listing.

ABC Electronics, Inc.   **1987—1989**
Aurora, Illinois
Manufacturer of First Alert home smoke detector and industrial fire alarm systems

- Engineering group leader for industrial fire alarm systems.
- Developed and guided a product through Underwriters Laboratories, and three similar approval agencies in Canada, Germany and Denmark. Visited the European agencies.

<u>**XYZ Electronics**</u>   **1972-1987**
Chicago, Illinois
<u>Design and manufacture of television receivers for Sears</u>
<u>Roebuck</u>

- Managed a TV engineering department with 20 engineers and technical staff.
- Directed engineering of first solid state color television receiver from prototype through production.
- Reduced cost of production of color TV receivers, saving $200,000 in one year.
- Extensive research and development role included: UHF varactor tuner, sound, chroma, C.R.T. circuits, scan, high voltage, video, transistorization, computer simulation.

EDUCATION   **Illinois Institute of Technology**
- MBA (Elected Sigma Iota Epsilon)

Illinois Institute of Technology
- MSAA (Elected Sigma XI)
- BSEE

Midwest College of Engineering
- 1980 post-graduate microprocessor design course.
- Recent in-house courses: digital signal processor, effective communication, "Novations", career planning and counseling.

PROFESSIONAL
ACTIVITIES

- Registered Professional Engineer of State of Illinois
- Senior member I.E.E.E.
- Past chairman I.E.E.E. Consumer Electronics Society
- Former member I.E.E.E. TV Measurements Standards Committee

REFERENCES WILL BE FURNISHED UPON REQUEST.

Power Resume Tip

Leave at least one inch at the top of the page, and use one-inch margins around the other three borders as well. Never go smaller than a half-inch margin. Large margins create a pleasing, organized, uncluttered feeling and many employers use that space to make notes.

Make Your Resume *Work*

Eliminate Clutter and Confusion

"I like this resume because it's results-oriented," says Vicki Spina, who heads her own career consulting service in the Chicago area. "Stevens has made effective use of white space and boldfaced heads. The type is clean and very readable."

Also, Spina says, the summary is interesting. "It draws the reader in," she adds. "In addition, there is good use of action words."

Stevens's resume, reprinted from Spina's book, *Getting Hired in the '90s*, covers a number of years and several jobs, yet the information is organized in a neat, almost understated way to ensure that there is no clutter or confusion.

Vicki Spina
Corporate Image

Vicki Spina is the owner of Corporate Image, a career consulting service in Palatine, Ill. She is the author of *Getting Hired in the '90s* and the newly released *Success 2000*, from which leading magazines have published excerpts. Spina presents seminars, workshops and consultations based on her books. She has been featured as a career strategist on CNBC television and most recently appeared on NBC's *Today* show.

Spina has an ongoing career column on the Internet at http://world.hire.com

Her e-mail address is http://www.sbt.net/spina

Samuel Stevens
519 Hartland Avenue
Bartlett, IL 60103   (708) 724-8367

SUMMARY/HIGHLIGHTS

Proactive team administrator with a proven track record in Human Resources and Marketing

Implemented corrective action plan resulting in retention of a $1,000,000 national account.

Streamlined personnel staff saving $50,000 in employee compensation annually.

Orchestrated most successful United Way Campaign in company history.

Reduced operating expenses by 20% (annual savings of over $100,000).

EDUCATION

Bachelor of Science Degree/Marketing
University of Wisconsin–1977
Professional Human Resource Certification Program–1993

PROFESSIONAL HISTORY

XYZ Management Group   7/92 to 8/93
Business Development Consultant

Project manager for successful recruitment selection campaigns with Fortune 500 Companies including: M/M Mars, Sears, Advo Systems Inc.

- Rebuilt a faltering facilities staffing program through effective management of human resources, daily operations and client servicing.

Risk Insurers Inc.   6/86 to 7/92
Regional Personnel Manager (400 employees)

Effectively managed a staff of 25 for a 10-office region with P/L of $1,000,000.

- Designed and implemented a flexible benefits plan which improved insurance coverage and saved company $5,000 in annual premiums.
- Established an effective college recruitment program which attracted top-quality employees and enhanced overall company productivity.
- Developed and conducted innovative training programs resulting in improved employee/manager morale and reduction of turnover by 20%.

Family Group Insurance   5/83 to 6/86
Branch Personnel/Office Manager (100 employees)

Autonomy for re-organizing staffing and employee relation programs. Instrumental in creating a team environment and establishing effective communication channels.

- Initiated employee discussion groups which identified productivity problems. Recommended appropriate solutions to management which were implemented, resulting in improved employee relations and company profitability.
- Recruited and hired an additional 20% staff in 90-day period.

Echo Shoe Manufacturing Company   1/80 to 5/83
Personnel Manager

Organized a start-up personnel department for 75 non-union staff employees. Coordinated activities of payroll, accounting and support services to insure smooth operations.

ABC Department Stores   9/77 to 1/80
Personnel Manager

- Rapidly promoted from Executive Trainee to Assistant Buyer to Employment Interviewer and Personnel Manager in less than three years.

COMMUNITY ACTIVITIES _____

Active Member/Society for Human Resource Management, 1987 to present
International Foundation of Employee Benefit Plans
Elected Chairman United Way Effectiveness Council, 1991-1992

ADDITIONAL TRAINING/SKILLS

Computer literate on PC-based Human Resource Programs
Work Force Diversity 2000
Employment Law in Illinois

Power Resume Tip

Pepper your resume with results-oriented accomplishments that spell B-E-N-E-F-I-T-S to employers. If your resume reads like a job description, you've got work to do.

Where Should I Shine My Spotlight?

Focus on Education, Stability and Accomplishments

"There are so many styles and techniques in resume writing that people often become confused and overwhelmed," says Ken Cowan, president of Cowan Search Group. "Professionals provide countless unique and different suggestions. So it is with this in mind that we provide Steven Giambrok's resume."

The recruitment specialist selected this resume because it effectively incorporates three important areas he consistently looks for in a person's background: education, stability and, most importantly, accomplishments. Steven covers all of them in a clear, concise and powerful method.

The Summary of Qualifications, which shows *why* Steven is the regional sales director, is supported throughout the resume with specific accomplishments for each of his previous positions with the company. He offers detailed statistics and numbers, providing evidence of success and leadership. It's obvious that Steven is an organized achiever. The use of bullets, including the awards received for each career advancement, is a simple, eye-catching method to highlight his consistent development.

"Steven's resume also provides a brief sentence which describes his current company," adds Cowan. "The sentence clearly informs the reader about the company's size and specialty. This technique, which should be used more often, helps the reader get involved and understand more of the candidate's background."

The general appearance of the resume is clean, simple and to the point. It has a smooth balance between descriptive phrases and bullet outline points, which helps the reader glide gracefully through it.

"This resume effectively utilizes the candidate's strengths, demonstrates them simply and, most importantly, holds the reader's attention," says Cowan. "The reader is left remembering that this candidate is an achiever and a consistent performer."

Ken Cowan
President, Cowan Search Group

Ken Cowan is president of Cowan Search Group, an employment recruitment company specializing in sales, marketing and sales management. Cowan Search Group assists advertising agencies, media companies, high-tech organizations and Fortune 500 companies in matching top-quality sales/marketing professionals with company needs.

The recruitment specialist has an extensive background in advertising sales and marketing. Before starting Cowan Search Group, he earned more than 50 achievement awards for sales, management and sales training. As a frequent speaker at universities, civic organizations and seminars, Cowan demonstrates techniques regarding hiring, training, marketing and salesmanship.

Steven Mark Giambrok
166 East Shore Lane
Lakedon, Virginia 21601
(603) 464 – 6281

CAREER OBJECTIVE: A challenging and responsible **Sales Management** position with an emphasis on building and directing a "high performance" sales team.

SUMMARY OF QUALIFICATIONS

Regional Sales Director with significant experience in managing large sales teams in various geographical territories. Known for analytical, problem solving and decision making skills. Special ability to teach, train and motivate associates as well as effective leadership and team building skills. Communicate effectively with clients and management on all levels.

PROFESSIONAL EXPERIENCE

Advertising Publications, Inc., Delta, Arizona   1985 - 1996

Advertising Publications, a division of BUC International with annual sales of over $2 Billion, is a publishing, advertising, fundraising and promotional organization with annual sales in excess of $200 M.

SIGNIFICANT ACHIEVEMENTS

- Achieved average revenue growth of 20%
- Increased operating profit by 300%, reduced expenses by 20%
- Piloted a plan to streamline the region, reduce cost and increase profit by $500,000
- Completed restructuring of region, hired and trained 4 new district and branch managers

REGIONAL DIRECTOR: Ft. Lauderdale, Florida (1995 – 1996)

Providing sales revenue, optimizing sales performance, reducing costs and profit and loss. Managed and directed the activities of 10 branch and district sales offices and 25 employees in Florida, Georgia and Louisiana. Annual territory sales were in excess of $5.5 Million.

REGIONAL MANAGER: Ft. Lauderdale, Florida (1993 – 1995)
- Regional Manager of the Year, 1994
- Best Sellers Circle, 1993, 1994, 1995

BRANCH MANAGER: Ft. Lauderdale, Florida (1992 – 1993)
- Branch Manager of the Year, 1993
- Best Sellers Circle, 1992
- Grand Champion City, Ft. Lauderdale, Florida, 1993

DISTRICT MANAGER: Ft. Lauderdale, Florida (1990 – 1992)
- District Manager of the Year, 1992
- Most Improved City, Ft. Lauderdale, Florida, 1991

DISTRICT MANAGER: Washington, D.C. (1987 – 1990)

SENIOR ACCOUNT EXECUTIVE: Washington, D.C. (1986 – 1987)
- Account Executive of the Year, 1986

ACCOUNT EXECUTIVE: Washington, D.C. (1985 – 1986)

M&M Limited, London, England   1980 – 1984
CONFECTIONARY CONSULTANT

Detailed and sold confectionery products to convenience stores, grocers and wholesalers.
- Special Achievement Award, 1983

EDUCATION
Bachelor of Science Degree, Business Administration
University of Dayton, Dayton, Ohio

Don't Leave Your Resume at the Door

Follow-up and Networking Should Be Part of Your Plan

As human resources manager for DowBrands, Rick Field has seen it all. Take for example the Christmas card with the sender's resume printed inside, or the cover letter that read like the script of an interview between Field and the sender, complete with salary discussion. Field sees up to 40 resumes a day, so while a novel approach may separate a candidate from the clutter, it still has to deliver in content.

"The first thing I look for is if people are familiar with the company and what we do," he says. "It bothers me when applicants don't even know what business we're in. They don't do their research, and they essentially tell me that in the cover letter."

When it comes to the resume, Field likes to see all the information on one page, with education listed first. He looks for ties to his geographic location. "I like candidates to have some reason besides the job for coming to Indiana," he says.

In the Experience section, he appreciates use of bullets to highlight information and prefers to see time spent on the job listed in years, not months, unless the experience was a special, short-term assignment. "I'm more impressed with breadth of assignments with one company than breadth of assignments with several," he says.

"Make sure you have a way for the employer to get in touch with you," Field stresses. "If you've listed your home phone number, use an answering machine. Nothing drops you to the bottom of the barrel faster than when you can't be reached." Follow-up is essential. Ask for feedback: Did my resume get your attention? Even though you don't have a job available right now, would you give me some advice? Department supervisors and hiring managers appreciate someone who makes an effort.

If your resume *does* land you an interview, Field suggests letting the employer know the competencies you're bringing to the table, such as initiative, leadership, interpersonal effectiveness and teamwork. For recent college graduates with little or no job experience, demonstrate your abilities through school activities.

The key to success is networking. "A lot more attention is paid to those who know people in the company and understand the business," he advises. "I heard about Gwen from three or four others in the company before she called me. Her resume is an excellent example of organization. It's on one page, it's succinct, it's nice to look at, it shows what she's done and what she's capable of doing. The various locations are explained by the fact that her husband is in the military and is frequently transferred."

Gwen's goal was to obtain a part-time marketing position to complement her "job" as mother of two girls, and it worked. She currently is a marketing research/marketing consultant for a small firm in Indianapolis.

Rick A. Field
Human Resources Manager, DowBrands

Rick Field is human resources manager for DowBrands, a subsidiary of Dow Chemical Company. DowBrands, headquartered in Indianapolis, produces and markets products such as Ziploc plastic bags, Saranwrap and Spray 'N Wash. During his 24 years with the company, Field has worked in sales, marketing, consumer promotion, trade promotion, information systems, packaging and human resources.

GWEN A. DAVIS
33 Winding Way South
Indianapolis, IN 46220
(317) 555-2333

SUMMARY STATEMENT

Professional with extensive experience implementing projects, leading financial analyses and creating business plans. Expertise in food/ingredient industry. MBA with marketing concentration.

EDUCATION

1990-1992

J.L. KELLOGG GRADUATE SCHOOL OF MANAGEMENT
NORTHWESTERN UNIVERSITY   Chicago, IL
Master of Management, The Managers' Program, December, 1992.
- Concentrations in Marketing and International Business.

1983-1987

UNIVERSITY OF NOTRE DAME   Notre Dame, IN
Bachelor of Business Administration, with Honors, May, 1987.
- Concentration in Finance.
- Honors: Seven semesters Dean's List, Beta Gamma Sigma.
- Activities: Captain of Dancin' Irish, Business Advisory Council.

EXPERIENCE

1993-1996

Independent Consultant   Denver, CO
- Designed and authored business plans to raise funds for companies in the start-up and expansion phases such as Wilson Bakery and Mountain Food Distributors.

Community Service Volunteer
- Elected 1st Vice President (1995-96) and Member-at-Large (1994-95) for the Adams Air Force Base Officers' Wives' Club, a scholarship and charitable association.
- Published quarterly newsletter for Notre Dame Club of Denver.

1991-1992

BURTON CORPORATION   Chicago, IL
Senior Financial Analyst
- Spearheaded long term planning, annual budgeting and quarterly forecasting for company's two top-selling products in the midst of a corporate reorganization, resulting in a streamlined operation.
- Acted independently as sales force's sole financial support during customer contract negotiations; credited with retaining customers.
- Selected to receive "Special Award for 1991" in recognition of outstanding achievement.

1990-1991

BUCKINGHAM, INC.   Palatine, IL
Financial Analyst
- Designed and implemented computerized volume, sales and profit reporting and analysis for Consumer Products Division and Professional Markets Group.
- Conducted new product and capital project feasibilty studies.

1987-1990

ELSON MARTIN, INC.   Bloomington, IL
Senior Financial Consultant
- Prepared and presented business proposals to potential clients regarding firm's services.
- Summarized costs and damages associated with business disputes such as bankruptcy, utility regulation and product liability cases.

REFERENCES

Available upon request.

A Resume That Achieved Great Results

"A .300 Batting Average"

"This resume for a chemical marketing professional generated a response rate of 30 percent when it was used to answer employment ads," notes Charles F. Albrecht, former president of Drake Beam Morin, Inc., the world's largest career consulting firm.

"The one-paragraph summary begins by highlighting three major areas of success," points out Albrecht. He says that this number is just right. "One accomplishment area would make the resume too limiting. Seven or eight might communicate lack of focus or cause the reader to believe that the candidate is exaggerating her accomplishments."

Albrecht notes that "throughout the resume, the candidate backs up her statement in the Summary that she is a results-oriented, self-motivated, award-winning marketing professional. For instance, she was a three-time award winner in one environment and had a success ratio 2.5 times the company average in another."

In addition, this candidate's career progression is nicely highlighted. "The most impressive and greatest number of accomplishments are listed under the most recent position," he adds. "And the candidate did not waste valuable space with early accomplishments in an entry-level position."

Albrecht also points out that the candidate's accomplishment statements are "full of qualifiers: actual amounts of sales and revenue increases, cost savings and time frames. The candidate projects an image of a person who gets quantifiable results quickly."

And this resume did the same!

Charles F. Albrecht, Jr.
Former President, Drake Beam Morin, Inc.

Drake Beam Morin, Inc., is the world's largest career consulting firm. With more than 100 U.S. and international offices, the firm assists more than 200,000 candidates each year in constructing their resumes. Charles Albrecht, Jr., most recently served as president of the company and before that was responsible for DBM's operations and sales in the Eastern U.S. and DBM's Key Account Program.

LISA M. FOYT

1234 Lake Avenue
Ringwood, NJ 07456
201-555-7626

SUMMARY

Twelve years of diversified experience and success in sales, marketing and technical service with a technical background in chemistry. Results-oriented, self-motivated, award-winning marketing professional.

Strengths include:

Direct Sales	Troubleshooting
Market/Product Analysis	Quality Management
Project Management	Program Administration
Strategy Development	Personal Computer Skills

EXPERIENCE

THE MIDWEST CHEMICAL COMPANY, Chicago, IL   1990-1996

Senior Marketing Representative

Represented company in technical sales and marketing for new business venture. Responsible for development and implementation of marketing strategies and programs.

Conceived, developed and administered several advertising, distributor and sales support programs, resulting in sales increase from $140M to $1.2MM.

Created, as member of special task force, initial strategic business plan leading to the acquisition of $30MM company.

Sold and managed comprehensive maintenance savings project for client company, resulting in over a three-year period in savings of $500M to client and revenues of $300M to Midwest Chemical.

Within 12-week period, managed launch of new product line, including generation of product inventory and literature.

Coordinated annual three-day training seminar leading to signing of $400M per year distributor.

Reduced out-of-stock complaints 90% by conceiving, programming and instituting a LOTUS 1-2-3 spreadsheet program to guide manufacturing planning.

RAYMOND TECHNICAL, INC., Newark, DE   1988-1990

Marketing Representative

Marketed and developed business for $7MM, 140 member consulting and engineering firm specializing in structural, chemical, environmental engineering and construction management.

> Proposed and conducted marketing research project identifying top growth markets and local area prospects.

> Planned and performed business development campaign resulting in success ratio 2.5 times company average, achieving $1.7MM in revenues from 17 successful projects.

HARRIS SERVICE & SUPPLIES, INC., Philadelphia, PA   1986-1988

Technical Sales Engineer

Designed, specified and sold custom-designed state-of-the-art systems, primarily to biomedical market.

> Proposed and sold $250M of equipment and service contracts, increasing sales by 30%.

ESSEX WATER, Philadelphia, PA   1983-1986

Accounts Manager

Managed 110 accounts in three-county, $300M territory. Supplied technical advice and support on industrial water treatment programs.

> Increased sales by 10% per year. Three-time award winner for top salesperson of quarter.

DCM, Pittsburgh, PA   1980-1983

Field Representative

Supplied lab and field chemistry support and training for water treatment accounts.

EDUCATION

B.S., Chemistry—University of Pittsburgh—1980
Computer Programming Minor

Power Resume Tip

Show your resume to friends, family members or trusted co-workers, preferably those familiar with your skills. They may be able to remind you of accomplishments or skills you have overlooked, or help with organization and content problems.

The Wired World of Job Searching

A 24-Hour Web Resume

"The World Wide Web is playing a bigger role in the job-search process as more and more companies go online," says Rebecca Smith of eResumes & Resources, an online resource for preparing, posting and promoting electronic resumes.

"This option provides new self-marketing opportunities in an increasingly competitive job market," she adds. "The key is in knowing how technology contributes to the resume development process in a way that best suits your needs. A Web resume may be just the thing if you have the kind of profession, such as a consultant, publisher, attorney or freelance graphic artist for example, where people come to you."

A Web resume is posted in one location on the Web, where interested employers and recruiters can view it 24 hours a day. It is most effective when used in combination with other self-marketing techniques in a coordinated job-search campaign. Web resumes employ a unique set of design strategies. Smith offers these tips that will assist you in capturing and holding your viewer's attention:

- Provide an obvious way to contact you. Many recruiters like an address and phone number in addition to a hyperlink to your e-mail address.

- Establish hyperlinks at the beginning to important categories within your resume, including specialized training and certifications. Provide hyperlinks to let the viewer jump back to the top of the page or to a major section of your resume. Use them to support, not distract. Adding a hyperlink to an employer's Web site will have the viewer wandering through that site, where he or she will likely lose interest in returning to your resume.

- Provide a keyword summary to give viewers the opportunity to assess your skills and qualifications at a glance. Two rules you can apply to keyword selection and presentation: 1) Limit the number of keywords to 25-35; and 2) Prioritize their order the same way you would prioritize information in your resume.

- Keep your resume current. The nature of the Internet is that information is updated daily. Outdated information is passed over for more current information.

- Keep the resume to a single Web page. If a recruiter finds your resume interesting, it will be printed anyway. Multiple pages make printing time-consuming, since the recruiter would have to open each page and print it separately.

Rebecca Smith
eResumes & Resources

Rebecca Smith has been monitoring career trends and computer technology for the past 10 years, with as many years' experience in personnel management. Her popular Web site, eResumes & Resources (http://www.eresumes.com), was featured in the *San Jose Mercury News* and Joyce Lain Kennedy's syndicated *Careers* column. Smith believes that today's job searching is about managing continuous employment opportunities, and that Internet technology plays a key role in that process. She currently writes a unique interactive online job search column for *Computer Bits* magazine (http://www.computerbits.com) that explores this theme.

Smith offers this additional information: A Web resume is a page on the Web containing hyperlinks, which consist of "clickable" text created in HTML (Hypertext Markup Language). Clicking on a hyperlink initiates a series of actions. The most common are linking to another part of the same page or to another page using a URL (Uniform Resource Locator). A URL specifies a page's location on the Internet.

Keep in mind the terms "Internet" and "World Wide Web" are entirely different things. The Internet is a global network of computers that can communicate with each other, regardless of model of computer. The Web is a popular component of the Internet due to its graphical interface; it consists of more than 30 million documents linked together via hyperlinks.

Getting your resume on the Web requires a Web browser (a software program that runs on your computer and lets you view pages on the World Wide Web), an HTML converter application and Internet access. Popular Web browsers include Microsoft Internet Explorer and Netscape Navigator. Converter applications such as Microsoft Internet Assistant for Word or Novell Internet Publisher for WordPerfect let you create a Web resume without having to know HTML. Internet access requires a computer, a modem and an account with an Internet Service Provider.

The following three figures illustrate the top page view, middle page view and bottom page view of a one-page Web resume as it would appear on the Internet. Note the position of the scroll bar in each figure, indicating what part of the document is being viewed. Hyperlinks are indicated as underlined text.

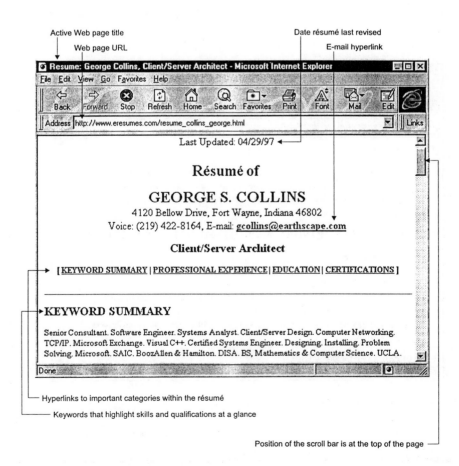

Convenient hyperlinks to important positions held under Professional Experience

A potentially distracting hyperlink to an employer's Web site

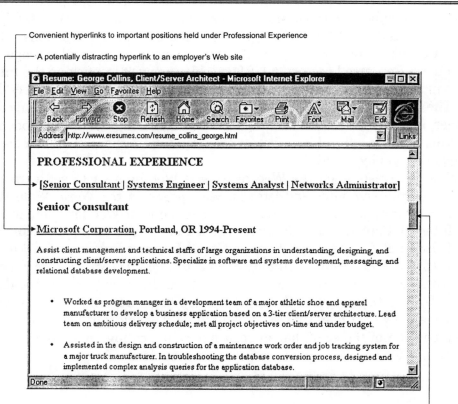

Position of the scroll bar is at the middle of the page

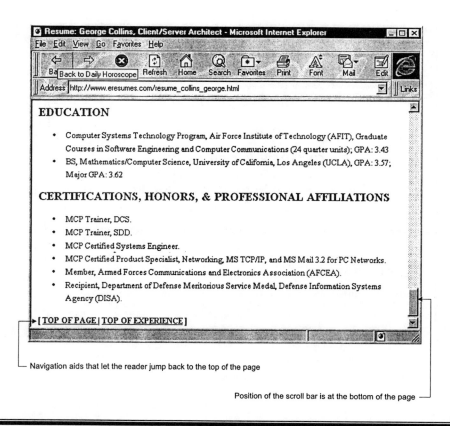

Navigation aids that let the reader jump back to the top of the page

Position of the scroll bar is at the bottom of the page

Power Resume Tip

Select white, off-white, ivory or buff-colored paper for your resume. These colors not only ensure easier readability, they're the least likely to inflame personal bias. You should also select a good-quality, medium-weight paper.

You Want to Do *What?*

Transferring Skills After 27 Years

"Larry came to me with the challenge of the year," says Debra O'Reilly, owner of A First Impression Resume Service in Bristol, Conn. "He had immense expertise as a CNC machinist, developed during a career spanning more than 25 years in the aerospace industry. It would have been a simple task to market those skills for any prospective employer. But that wasn't what he wanted."

Larry was tired of his career. Before his days as a machinist, he was a military police officer and served overseas in a secret assignment for a year. It was an exciting time, and he kept thinking about it. He wanted a resume for a job in the security field, perhaps even covert operations.

This single-page resume did the trick. Because Larry's long work history as a machinist was with a single employer, he and O'Reilly chose to use the top half of the page to describe Larry's transferable skills that made a career cross-over realistic for him. The summary presented skills, including "uniquely observant" and "highly disciplined," which were important to both kinds of work.

"Although Larry's only security experience was 27 years earlier, the summary included a brief (and eye-catching) description of it, exposing the reader to it within the first 30 seconds of reading time," O'Reilly explains.

Larry reported that this resume, accompanied with a brief cover letter, resulted in nearly a 100 percent response rate. He accepted a position as Director of Undercover Security Operations at a top-rated hotel in a major city.

Debra O'Reilly, CPRW
Owner, A First Impression Resume Service

Debra O'Reilly has, for seven years, successfully counseled resume and job-search clients nationwide from her Bristol, Conn., headquarters. She is a Certified Professional Resume Writer (CPRW) and an active member of the Professional Association of Resume Writers (PARW). Articles by O'Reilly have been published in *National Business Employment Weekly*, a *Wall Street Journal* publication, and in the PARW periodical, *Spotlight*. Her resume services are detailed at her Web site on the Internet at www.resumewriter.com

Lawrence Manly

123 Main Street
Anytown, USA 12345
(123) 456-7890

SUMMARY OF SKILLS:

- Over twenty-five years of comprehensive experience in a highly technical field, with expertise in machining and inspection techniques of extremely close-tolerance parts. Trained to be uniquely observant, attentive to detail, highly disciplined and self-reliant.

- Entrusted with fabrication and inspection of state-of-the-art, extremely expensive components with very tight tolerances, using state-of-the-art techniques. These parts are the highest-stressed components of the latest designs of jet engines, and are integral to achieving the highest standards of aviation safety.

- Skilled hands-on instructor, with proven leadership skills in training and motivating others. Designated departmental trainer, schooling both new and veteran employees on this precise, highly sensitive equipment.

- Military training in security-related activities; hand-selected for top-secret classification policing assignment overseas.

PROFESSIONAL EXPERIENCE:

4/67 - 9/94   PRATT & WHITNEY, Southington, CT
Certified CNC Machinist: Machines the major rotating parts of jet engines. Inspects every machined dimension, utilizing a state-of-the-art tracking process. Appointed sole departmental trainer on high-tech CNC vertical turret lathe.

- Received personal award for extraordinary effort in achieving high volume quota fulfillment.
- Earned attendance award for reliability and punctuality on the job.

EDUCATION: TUNXIS COMMUNITY-TECHNICAL COLLEGE, Farmington, CT
1985   **Associate's Degree**

PRATT & WHITNEY AIRCRAFT, Southington, CT
1992   **"Train the Trainer"**
1977   **Technical Training School**

MILITARY: U.S. Marine Corps
Military Police; L/Cpl.
1966   Honorable Discharge

COMMUNITY INVOLVEMENT:

1991 - 1994   Adjutant: American Legion

No Unnecessary Baggage

A Resume That Hits the Target

"Although there are many types of resumes from one page to 30 pages," says John J. Turnblacer, "I like this one because it is very simple, to the point, easy to follow and easy to read. All of the pertinent information is contained within this simple format, and superfluous words, such as 'references available upon request,' are excluded. In addition to being well-drafted, the resume is easy on the reader's eye."

Turnblacer is president of The Gabriel Group. He likes this jam-packed resume because "when you first look at it, you know exactly what the individual is—a sales and marketing executive."

He also notes that within the Professional Experience section, the companies and positions are very readable upon a quick scan.

"Achievements are well-highlighted with quantification, but not puffed out of proportion. The Education and Professional Training sections are presented in a straightforward manner, even though the candidate has no degree."

The candidate delivers a concise summary of accomplishments under the heading for each employer mentioned. These paragraphs are followed by an impressive list of succinctly stated achievements.

John J. Turnblacer
President, The Gabriel Group

John J. Turnblacer is based in Philadelphia with overall responsibility for this high-quality, full-service human resource consulting firm. He counsels top executives through the job-campaign process and advises client companies in planning human resource strategies and implementations.

Prior to joining The Gabriel Group, he held executive-level positions for ITT, Citicorp and Allied Signal, in operations, human resources and administration with global responsibilities.

Turnblacer is a member of the Society for Human Resource Management and has been a member of several state bars. He holds a J.D. degree from Chase College of Law and a B.S. from the University of Dayton. He sits on the Board of Aspen Health Services, chairs the Mentoring Partnership Advisory Board and serves on the Board of Strategic Alliance, Inc.

JOHN HENRY

275385 South Ardmore Road
Villanova, PA 19073

(h) 215-555-1234
(o) 215-555-5678

SALES/MARKETING EXECUTIVE

Over twenty-five years of top management experience in the domestic and international automobile, truck and construction equipment industries with extensive background in marketing, dealer development, and sales initiatives. Successful record of building national field organizations in parts and service as well as vehicle sales. Skilled in the preparation of operating plans and development of budgets and pricing analyses. A dynamic success-oriented manager who demands and gets the most from subordinates. Outstanding verbal and written communications skills.

PROFESSIONAL EXPERIENCE

JI CASE COMPANY Racine, WI   1991-1992
Division of Tenneco. Manufacturer of construction equipment; world-wide sales of $3.6 billion.

Regional Manager
Northeast US/Eastern Canada
Managed staff of 12, 90 dealers, responsible for marketing, dealer development, customer satisfaction, sales of $180 million.

- Reduced region inventory from $50 million to less than $3 million by utilizing selldown promotions and dealer incentives.
- Increased market share in an industry which was in a decline of 35-40%.
- Implemented procedures to promote customer service/satisfaction including assigning an individual at each dealership, utilizing customer surveys, encouraging district managers to follow-up on key accounts.
- Attained an "under budget" condition by initiating cost cuts in areas which did not affect sales or service.

SUBARU OF AMERICA Cherry Hill, NJ   1988-1991

Director - Market Development
Developed, coordinated and implemented national policies and procedures for the business management, dealer development and market planning departments. Objectives included increasing sales per outlet and enhancing the value of the franchise through upgrading existing dealers and appointing qualified new dealers in open points.

- Improved sales per outlet by designing and following "Blue print" for upgrading dealer performance. Tracked monthly, replaced dealers where performance was poor.
- Co-chaired committee for hiring and training entry level management trainees. Success of program led to 10 new Field District Sales Managers in 2 years.
- Developed and published Subaru Market Development Policy Manual containing national policies and procedures regarding franchise and representation issues. Approved by legal staff and top management. Remains in effect today.
- Created a confidential product book for new dealer solicitation.
- Developed regional marketing plans for the Midwest and California.

AMERICAN MOTORS CORPORATION Southfield, MI   1972-1988

Director - Field Sales Operations (1985-1988)
Directed a staff of 15 and a national field organization of 340; headquartered in 8 regional offices; serviced 1500 dealers; sales objectives 350,000 units and $3 billion annually.

- Improved productivity of field sales organization by over 50%.
- Attained all time monthly sales record of over 23,000 Jeep vehicles.
- Reduced plant inventory of 10,000 units in 2 months with "0% APR" incentive.
- Reviewed and approved all dealer co-op advertising with $15 million budget.

Director - Sales - Central/Southfield, MI (1982-1985)
                    - West/Denver, CO
Directed and supervised 200 personnel in 4 zones to accomplish sales, parts and service objectives for over 500 dealers. Chaired the California Marketing Committee responsible for developing and executing a special advertising and merchandising budget of $5 million.

- Coordinated the site selection and construction of three company-owned dealerships.
- Completed a successful launch of the Renault Alliance-1983 Motor Trend Car of the Year and Jeep Cherokee-1984 4x4 of the Year.
- Improved market share of Jeep in California.

Director - Jeep Marketing Southfield, MI (1981-1982)
Responsible for marketing, planning, advertising, sales promotion, product information and production control functions for Jeep vehicles in a brand manager marketing concept. Controlled a $40 million budget. Directed a staff of 12 and interfaced with Compton Advertising, sales and manufacturing personnel to develop monthly production controls.

- Increased sales of Jeep CJ by 45%.
- Designed and implemented a direct mail program for Jeep Grand Wagoneer which increased sales by 10%.
- Designed the launch of the XJ (Cherokee) Project.
- Developed the "Why buy a car when you can drive a Jeep" advertising campaign.

Director - Sales Operations Southfield, MI (1981)
Directed and supervised National Vehicle Distribution, Market Representation, Business Management and Dealer Relations Departments consisting of 54 personnel located in 3 plant locations and central office.

- Approved all dealer franchising actions including buy/sells, open points, terminations.
- Coordinated and integrated computer systems network between AMC and Renault in France for vehicle distribution.
- Managed the national dealer council and coordinated the annual meeting process.

Zone Manager Multiple AMC sites (1972-1980)

EDUCATION

Business Management Certificate *Northwood Institute*
Attending The Wharton School *University of Pennsylvania*
BBA Program Business Administration with a focus on Marketing

PROFESSIONAL TRAINING

Kepner, Tregoe--Executive Decision Program
Chrysler Corporation Quality Improvement Program (QIP)
Subaru Leadership Development Seminar
Training in TV and Radio Interview Techniques

MILITARY

US Navy Reserve 1959-1961
2nd Class Petty Officer, Destroyer duty, Pacific Fleet

Power Resume Tip

If you're going to print copies of your original resume, *don't* use the copy machine in your office, the library or your local drugstore. These machines are usually not very well-maintained. Your best bet is to use a commercial copy shop.

A Place for Bells and Whistles

When Repetition Bears Repeating

"Formatting, writing and layout should always be subordinate to strategy in developing an effective resume," says Mark Gisleson, a resume writer with more than 10,000 resumes and cover letters to his credit.

While he follows traditional resume formats, Gisleson says he also uses "cheap tricks, bells and whistles, inspired writing—and whatever works" to manipulate the reader—pulling him or her into the copy and creating a need to meet the person whose name is at the top of the page.

Gisleson is quick to point out that he uses key information over and over again in the sample resume. "In this case, the client's job experience was unrelated to her objective. It was important to promote her related skills since her intended audience was an anonymous government bureaucrat.

"Because government standard forms for hiring (SF-171s or OF-612s) are designed to be repetitious and exhaustive, I have found that you often need to hit federal bureaucrats over the head several times before you can get your point across."

He adds, "In this case, we began by listing skills appropriate to the position. In effect, we defined the job before ever mentioning the position of 'project manager.' A Related Experience section was then created to highlight her internship, which was directly related to the position. This job description gives examples of the skills mentioned in the summary, providing reinforcement.

"The final repetition comes in the Continuing Education section where the client's VA experience is trotted out again, this time in the form of on-the-job training."

Gisleson considers the artful use of repetition one of his most effective strategies.

As a final touch, Gisleson likes to use an Interests or Activities section to demonstrate client "physical fitness or concern about health, intellectual activity not related to work and just about anything that is a little different or unusual."

Mark Gisleson
Writer

Doing business as Gisleson Writing Services in St. Paul, Minn., Mark Gisleson has worked with more than 5,500 job seekers nationwide since 1988, writing resumes, letters, SF-171s/OF-612s and personal statements for applicants to graduate schools. A former manager for Professional Resume & Writing Services and Career-Pro, Gisleson has authored more than 60 articles and columns on various career development topics that can be accessed at his Web site at http://www.gisleson.com

KIMBERLY BROWN

1558 Albany, St. Paul, MN 55108
612 644-6408

SUMMARY *of* PROFESSIONAL QUALIFICATIONS

- Highly dedicated new graduate with well-developed communication and organizational skills; strong project management experience.
- Goal-oriented; able to make effective use of all available resources.
- Self-starter; works well independently or as member of a team.

EDUCATION

COLLEGE OF ST. JOSEPH, St. Benedict, MN
Bachelor of Arts Degree, May 1994
Liberal Studies major.

Advanced coursework taken in SCIENCE and MANAGEMENT:
- ▸ Microbiology · Chemistry · Anatomy
- ▸ Management · Marketing · Business

RELATED EXPERIENCE

VETERAN'S ADMINISTRATION HOSPITAL, St. Benedict, MN
Administrative Internship, February 1994 to May 1994

Reported to the Staff Assistant for Clinical Affairs.

Independently researched and designed a Total Quality Improvement directory which was approved and implemented by the hospital. This same directory was subsequently adapted for official use by the Nursing Program at St. Joseph's.

At the request of the Hospital Director, reviewed and analyzed the hospital's committee system, focusing on issues related to member participation, ability to implement change, and committee's status (regulation mandated, etc.).

EMPLOYMENT

CARSON PIRIE SCOTT, St. Benedict, MN
Sales Associate – SHOE DEPARTMENT, 1994 to Present

Provide immediate and attentive customer service, assisting with selections of moderate to better shoes and accessories.

Additional responsibilities include stocking, inventory, balancing cash registers and answering customer questions.

MONTGOMERY WARD, St. Benedict, MN
Sales Associate, 1990 to 1994

Worked with all facets of store sales from customer service to returns, as well as assisting with display set-ups and promotions.

Trained and supervised new personnel; functioned as assistant manager as necessary.

MIDWESTERN MECHANICAL, Blaine, MN
Janitor, 1989 to 1990

CONTINUING EDUCATION

VETERAN'S ADMINISTRATION: Ongoing training in VA administrative, staffing and committee structures, lines of communication and authority.

CARSON PIRIE SCOTT/MONTGOMERY WARD: On-the-job sales, merchandising, and customer service training.

COMMUNITY

Active participant in VISTO, a St. Joseph's sponsored service organization.

Assisted with a latchkey program at Kennedy Elementary, working with children in grades 1-5.

INTERESTS

- ▸ Vice President, St. John's/St. Joseph's Karate Club.
- ▸ Swimming, skiing and horseback riding.

More Than Just Buzz Words

The Person Behind the Technological Resume

"The challenge of a technical resume is that the job seeker must convey complex technical terminology while enabling the reader to appreciate that there is more to him or her than buzz words," says Pamela Brody, associate recruiter at The Guild Corporation. Many resumes do not convey areas of expertise, either by conveying too little information or, in some cases, stating too much.

A good resume allows a reader, at first glance, to obtain a general knowledge of one's background, and increase the probability of a face-to-face interview.

Danielle begins with her contact information, which includes her address, telephone number and, in keeping up with today's technology, her e-mail address.

Danielle's Tools and Technologies section functions as a synopsis of strengths. Its purpose is to allow the reader to understand the correlation between the candidate's background and the job opportunity. Not all must be this extensive: They can be as short as three sentences.

The Experience section should be in chronological order, placing emphasis on more recent experience, and consistent throughout. Danielle includes her company's name, dates worked, job title, a brief statement about what the company does, her roles on specific projects and the tools and technologies she used for the project.

Pamela Brody
The Guild Corporation

Pamela Brody is an associate recruiter with The Guild Corporation, a high-end technology recruiting firm. The Guild's clients are rapidly growing organizations working in the areas of information technology management consulting, data and telecommunications, as well as software product development. Prior to her employment at The Guild Corporation, Pamela was a recruiter in New York City for a retainer-based search firm specializing in financial operations.

DANIELLE PORTER

1100 Briarway Drive
Anywhere, VA 98474
Home (703) 555-1212/Work (703) 999-0000
dporter@TelcomW.com

EDUCATION

1996-Present	George Washington, Washington, D.C., M.S. Computer Science
1995	Boston College, Boston, Mass., B.S. Computer Science

CERTIFICATION CLASSES

UNIX, Perl, Verity Search 97

TOOLS AND TECHNOLOGIES

- Computer Platforms: Microsoft NT 4.0/3.51; Windows 95; Sun Solaris 2.5; HP Unix; NeXT; Macintosh

- Server Software: Web Server software, Microsoft IIS, O'reilly & Associates Website, Netscape; Enterprise Server, Oracle Website; Microsoft Back Office (NT 4.0/3.51, SQL Server 6.5, Exchange, SMS, IIS); Lotus Notes 4.0/4.5, Domino, InterNotes; Cognisoft Intellserv Information Profiling Software; Web Trends Server tracking and Statistics; Excite Search for Web Servers; Verity Search97: Information Server, Agent Server and Toolkit, and Information Spider; RTI NewsMachine and Web Adapter; Precept IPTV Video Servers; White Pine CU-SeeMe Video Servers

- Development Software: Microsoft Visual Studio 97; NetDynamics 2.0, 3.0; Cold Fusion 1.5, 2.0; BackWeb Push Technology, BALI Info-Pack Creation Software; Marimba Castanet Push Technology; Adobe PDF Exchange and Catalogue; Macromedia Director 5.0; Front Page; Hot Dog Pro; Photoshop 4.0

- Programming Languages: C/C++, Java/Java Script, PERL, HTML, Cold Fusion, and FORTRAN

EXPERIENCE

Telecomm Worldwide, Washington, D.C.   May 1996 to Present
Systems Analyst

Presently performs as a Systems Analyst responsible for Intranet development for a leading edge telecommunications firm: Project highlights include:

- Deployed, managed, and administered the network TW Library's website, the largest and most visited enterprise Intranet site within Telecomm Worldwide.

- Designed, developed, and implemented Corporate Intranet Search Site, using Verity Search 97 information retrieval tools. Aided in the development in TWÕs Intranet Catalogue application, "Site Finder."

- Created dynamic database driven sites using Cold Fusion, Perl, and Microsoft Active Server Pages, including several corporate news and HR sites.

- Set up Real-time news, document, and information profiling service for TW ExecutiveONE, using RTI News Machine, RTI Web Adapter, and Verity Search97.

- Developed several dynamic document repositories for research documents.

- Developed the TW Channel, a Web biased multimedia TV platform and scheduling application using Precept IPTV, and Cu-SeeMe Video Servers.

- Installed, configured, and maintained three Domains of over 20 Windows NT 4.0 servers and workstations. Maintained a Sun Sparc 20 running Solaris 2.5.

When the Letter is the Law

A Positive Presentation for a Paralegal

"This resume is brief, concise and provides all of the important information for the interviewer's perusal," says Marilyn Hammerle, administrator for the law firm Hall, Render, Killian, Heath & Lyman of Indianapolis, Ind.

"It uses only one page and provides a terrific amount of white space, making it attractive and reader-friendly," she adds. "It includes all of the key information to gain Megan Fischer an interview for a paralegal position."

The Education and Objective sections show Megan's interest in a paralegal career since she obtained an undergraduate degree before her paralegal studies and certification.

The Responsibilities category includes experience in the specific areas that are imperative for a litigation paralegal. The resume reflects Megan's 10 years' experience in a manner that confirms essential work assignments.

"In addition, the Awards and Interest sections point out Megan's personal characteristics to help determine if she will fit into the firm's culture," says Hammerle.

Marilyn Hammerle
Administrator, Hall, Render, Killian, Heath & Lyman

Marilyn Hammerle is a former president of the Indiana Association of Legal Administrators and is a member of the National Association of Legal Administrators. In her role as administrator, she has managed the human resources area of Hall, Render, Killian, Heath & Lyman for 16 years. The law firm has offices in Indiana and Kentucky and is a leading firm concentrating in health law in the United States.

MEGAN J. FISCHER

502 Rosewood Court
Cape Kyle, Arizona 46339
(371) 835-5389

1984 Michigan State University
Bachelor of Arts

University of Kansas
1986 Associates in Arts
(Paralegal Studies--Certified)

OBJECTIVE

To obtain a paralegal position in a stable and successful firm to utilize my experience and knowledge as a litigation paralegal to the highest extent.

PROFESSIONAL EXPERIENCE

Connor & Matthews, P.S.C.
3000 National City Bldg.
Frankfort, Kentucky 40202

1986 to 1992

Arnold, Kawaters & Holleman
2000 American Tower
Phoenix, Arizona 47166

1992 to present

RESPONSIBILITIES

- Client contact
- File organization
- Document drafting
- Participation of discovery
  Drafting discovery requests and responses; deposition notices; deposition questions; affidavits; document control
- Trial preparation and attendance
  Extract and organize exhibits; prepare trial notebooks; communicate with client, witnesses and experts; assist in jury selection; maintain trial notebook and exhibits and coordinate witnesses
- Assist in drafting bankruptcy pleadings

AWARDS

- President-Gold Key Academic Honor Society
- Member-Alpha Lamda Delta-Phi Sigma National College Scholastic Honorary Societies
- Dean's List-(Six Semesters)
- Valedictorian of Senior Class 1979

INTERESTS

- Tennis, Water-skiing, and Reading

References and Writing Samples Available Upon Request

Delivering a Powerful Punch

A 'Power' Resume is a Dynamic Self-Marketing Piece

"In today's highly competitive environment, your resume must be a marketing tool of the 21st century, not a chronological history of your career," says Beverly Harvey, Certified Professional Resume Writer (CPRW). "It must be succinct, sharp and display exceptional communication skills. It must deliver evidence that you understand what affects the prospective employer's bottom line."

Harvey explains that your *accomplishments* are the benefits you have to offer the employer...and you must deliver them aggressively. She says it's important to provide an overview of responsibilities, but you also need to include as many *quantifiable* achievements as possible.

"Use numerous action words to develop the perception of high energy, innovativeness, effectiveness, leadership and outstanding expertise," she advises. "Remember, competition is fierce, and you must position yourself as the ultimate expert in your field."

Donald Land came to Harvey for resume help after he was requested to take early retirement due to downsizing initiatives. Although Land's resume is two pages, it is still succinct, easy to read and, most importantly, positions him as an expert in the industry while providing solid achievements that demonstrate his understanding and knowledge of corporate goals and missions.

Beverly Harvey
Certified Professional Resume Writer (CPRW)

Beverly Harvey, headquartered in Orange City, Fla., consults with professionals nationwide in the development of resumes, career search and marketing programs and interviewing techniques. She has been published in *Gallery of Best Resumes for Two-Year Degree Graduates* and was featured in the *Daytona Beach News-Journal*. Harvey earned her designation as Certified Professional Resume Writer in 1993 through the Professional Association of Resume Writers. She regularly holds training seminars for colleges, universities, fraternities, various businesses groups and corporations.

DONALD LAND

(904) 775-0916 • Juniper Lane • Deltona, Florida 32700

CAREER PROFILE

Well-qualified professional with a strong background in general management, operations, human relations and communications. Consistently successful in developing innovative strategies to improve teamwork and safety. Strong accomplishments in delivering customer-perceived value. Areas of expertise include:

- Transportation Industry
- Ramp Functions/Policies/Procedures
- Vehicle Maintenance Programs
- Security Operations/Monitoring
- Strategic Operational Planning
- Productivity Improvements
- Contingency Planning
- Field Operations
- Budget Administration/Accountability

- Public Relations/Customer Service/Sales
- Team Development/Motivation
- In-house Training/Instruction
- Personnel Administration/EEO & AAP
- Union and Non-Union Employee Supervision
- Liaison with Government Authorities
- In-house Audits
- Startup Operations/Organization
- OSHA Compliance

CAREER ACHIEVEMENTS

- Simultaneously increased Federal Express pick-up stops and pick-up efficiencies from 90 to 100%.
- Reduced critically-consequential paperwork errors which earned Federal Express' #1 ranking for the southern region.
- Ensured error-free pickups and deliveries for space program resulting in recognition by senior management.
- Successfully maintained outbound freight on scheduled aircraft without departure delay in spite of a power outage during peak rush hour.
- Assisted team in achieving a record number of check rides to provide statistical feedback.
- Increased reload productivity by improving pull times by 15 minutes per hour, exceeding all goals.
- Coordinated District Operations Managers Workshops for Federal Express.
- Successfully opened, coordinated, and managed a new station for Eastern Airlines including all phases, of research, acquisition, and setup.
- Consistently exceeded corporate expectations for leadership, management and human relations skills.

EXPERIENCE

A MAJOR EXPRESS MAIL CORPORATION   04/88 to Present

Operations Manager – Jacksonville, Florida – 04/90 to Present
Supervise, coordinate and control pick-up and delivery operations for station. Select, train, develop, motivate, and audit a team of approximately 25-35. Assist in administration of annual operating budget. Perform overall audit on packages in-house and on vehicles. Inspect facilities and vehicles to ensure company image and safe working environment. Provide security for FEC and customer properties. Supervise and coordinate all ground operations relating to the operational interface between aircraft and the station. Ensure compliance with OSHA regulations.

Operations Manager – Philadelphia, Pennsylvania – 04/88 to 04/90
Managed and lead a team of 25 in all phases of daily operations for Philadelphia station.

A MAJOR AIRLINE CARRIER   01/69 to 04/88

Manager Operational Security – Miami International Airport, Florida – 09/87 to 04/88
Managed entire operational security program including performance accountability, security
equipment maintenance programs, FAA approved training programs, violations, and signage.
Served as liaison with FAA and State Department. Coordinated scheduling of equipment at
screening points, passenger screening, point manning, alerts and warnings.

Manager of Departure Services – Miami International Airport, Florida – 03/87 to 09/87
Coordinated departure activity, personnel and administration. Supervised approximately
160 non-management employees and seven line supervisors.

Manager Sales/Services – McGhee Tyson Airport, Tennessee – 12/85 to 03/87
Managed entire airport operation. Handled all contract services for three major carriers.

Manager Sales/Services – Memphis Shelby County Airport, Tennessee – 10/84 to 12/85
Researched, set-up, coordinated, and opened new facility. Managed all phases of operations.

Passenger/Departure Service Supervisor – Orlando International Airport, Florida – 06/80 to 10/84
Supervised daily activities of flight operations, passenger services, and personnel administration.

Supervisor of Departure/Passenger Services – LaGuardia Airport, New York – 11/71 to 06/80
Supervised departures, ticket counter, ramp and passenger service activities at the central terminal
and air shuttle facilities.

Customer Service Agent – Philadelphia International Airport, Pennsylvania – 01/69 to 11/71
Coordinated ticket counter and assisted customers.

EDUCATION
A MAJOR EXPRESS MAIL CORPORATION
Quality Training in TQA/QAT – 1991
International Information Coordinator Program – 1989
Driver Instructor Training Program – 1989
Courier Training Program – 1989
Safety Management Course – 1988
Management Practices – 1988
Management Development Program – 1988
FAMIS Training Program – 1988

WILSON LEARNING
Managing Interpersonal Relationships – 1988

GEORGIA STATE UNIVERSITY
Problem Solving and Decision Making – 1988

MILITARY
United States Navy – Petty Officer

Power Resume Tip

The best method for producing your resume is to use a personal computer to create it and a high-quality computer printer to reproduce it. This will allow you to make any changes instantly, and easily update or modify it to respond to specific job opportunities.

Wearing the Old School Ties

Putting Your Best Foot Forward

A recent *New Yorker* cartoon depicts a gravestone on which is inscribed something like: "John B. Rutherford. Princeton, 1926-1930."

Indeed, some of us do place too much importance on *where* someone went to school, but it's easy to see why this candidate would list his degrees and the institutions at which he attained them right at the top. He immediately positions himself as a scientist with a terrific aptitude for management.

What's more, the resume, by being concise and packed with a great deal of information in just one page, demonstrates that the candidate probably is someone "respected for ability to communicate," as stated in the Personal Qualifications section, points out John Dugan, president of JH Dugan & Associates.

"This resume is concise, historical and thorough without being verbose," Dugan says. "It is to the point, informative and convincing."

He adds that you should position or target your resume for each presented opportunity by using the exact title or relational description in each Objective section.

"You may have multiple resumes, but now the reader knows your intentions," he says. "Don't be vague by being everything to everyone. And don't use 'or.'"

Note that the candidate used a smaller typeface to pack a great deal of information onto one page.

While this might have some drawbacks, "it saves readers time and insures that all of this candidate's impressive credentials are read at almost a single glance," says Dugan.

John Dugan
President, JH Dugan & Associates

JH Dugan & Associates is an executive search firm specializing in the plastics industry and is located in Carmel, Calif. Its president, John Dugan, is past chairman of the National Association of Executive Recruiters and has been director for 10 years.

MBA, Harvard Business School
BS, Chemical Engineering, MIT

objective   Industrial Marketing/Sales

background   General Manager with experience in product management, market research, OEM
summary   and distributor sales and manufacturing.

personal   Known as a quick learner with strong analytical and interpersonal skills. Respected
qualifications   for ability to communicate with all levels involved in delivering an industrial product
to market—from design and production to the customer's management, engineering
and purchasing staff.

business
experience   **CUNNINGHAM INDUSTRY, INC.**   **NEWARK, NEW JERSEY**
1994-1995   Privately owned contractor of hazardous chemical waste cleanup services in the
Northeast. Sales of $2.5 million, with 36 employees at two sites.

General Manager. P&L responsibility with authority for all nonaccounting aspects of
the business including direction of the New Jersey branch office. Management
responsibility for oil spill cleanup contracts in the Caribbean Basin and the Port of
New York & New Jersey, serving two oil company cooperatives.
•Reduced losses by $1.0 million from 1993 levels.
•Reduced employee turnover through improved consistency and fairness in
   personnel practices.
•Reduced and hired New Jersey branch manager and operations supervisor, and
   salespersons for both operations. Succeeded in attracting highly qualified individuals
   in spite of extremely limited budget.
•Negotiated all company cleanup contracts, including major subcontract for EPA.
•Changed suppliers for major product line, resulting in margin increase from 25% to 45%.
•Prepared 1995 annual plan and budget—a first for the business.

1991-1994   **BAKER CORPORATION**   **BOSTON, MASSACHUSETTS**
Privately held manufacturer of automotive interior parts, with annual sales of more
than $50 million.

Product/Account Manager. Market development responsibility for nonautomotive
and direct sales responsibility for Chrysler and American Motors accounts,
representing $1.5 million in sales and $400,000 in tooling.
•Established product line strategy, including pricing, distribution, packaging and
   promotion for the company's first nonautomotive product.
•Negotiated numerous price increases due to engineering changes, totaling
   approximately 100% by six months into production.
•Prepared and presented technical reviews for customer engineering staff; succeeded
   in getting product specifications revised to meet actual production capabilities.
•Planned and directed company booth at industry trade shows.

1986-1989   **INDY COMPANY**   **CAMBRIDGE, MASSACHUSETTS**
Process Engineer. Responsible for process improvement, design and controls.
Estimated product costs and production standards. Coordinated production of test
products for marketing and product development.

education
1989-1991   **HARVARD GRADUATE SCHOOL**
OF BUSINESS ADMINISTRATION   **BOSTON, MASSACHUSETTS**
Master of Business Administration. General management curriculum with emphasis
on marketing and operations. Summer job in 1990 as a marketing consultant to an
aftermarket automotive parts manufacturer.

1983-1986   **MASSACHUSETTS INSTITUTE**
OF TECHNOLOGY   **CAMBRIDGE, MASSACHUSETTS**
Bachelor of Science in Chemical Engineering; varsity skiing, four years; co-captain
senior year.

A Change in Direction

Emphasizing Experience Related to New Goals

After five years in the work force, Kristen Harris was ready for a career change.

"Since graduating college, Kristen held three jobs in the fields of systems programming and analysis," said Julie Adair King, president and owner of Julie King Creative, Inc. and author of *The Smart Woman's Guide to Resumes and Job Hunting* and *The Smart Woman's Guide to Interviewing and Salary Negotiation*.

"In all three jobs, one of Kristen's responsibilities was to train company employees on how to use various computer systems. This experience caused her to rethink her original long-term goal, which was to be an MIS department manager. She so enjoyed the teaching aspects of her jobs that she decided to move into the training field. There's an opening for a systems trainer in her company, and she's going to apply."

As a result, Kristen created a Skills Summary that emphasizes her training background. "In addition," notes King, "she makes a point to include the fact that she performed training in all of her positions."

The systems trainer position for which she is applying requires a broad knowledge of many different types of hardware, software and programming languages, so Kristen includes a list of those systems in which she is proficient.

Julie Adair King
President, Julie King Creative, Inc.

Julie Adair King is co-author of *The Smart Woman's Guide to Resumes and Job Hunting* and author of *The Smart Woman's Guide to Interviewing and Salary Negotiation*. King is president and owner of Julie King Creative, Inc., a marketing and creative services corporation based in Indianapolis. She frequently talks about career and job hunting issues on radio and TV and leads workshops and lectures. King is also a contributing writer to various publications.

KRISTEN B. HARRIS
3234 Seneca Drive
Houston, TX 77082
(713) 555-2310

Skills Summary
Five years experience in system analysis and programming for international transportation and energy corporations. Strong background in user training and support documentation. Experience in major programming languages, operating hardware and software.

Experience
8/95-present   Global Airlines, Houston
Senior Systems Analyst, Sales Administration and Program Development.
Create database programming to meet management and field-sales information needs.
Design and implement sales systems at company's regional technical centers.
Train sales staff on use of new programs.
Developed voice-automation system that increased telemarketing department productivity and allowed 15% staffing reduction.

6/92-8/95   World Oil Company, Houston
Purchasing Systems Analyst, Corporate Procurement and Materials Management.
Promoted from Systems Analyst position in June 1994.
Programmed management-reporting systems for purchasing department.
Served as liaison between system users and technical support group.
Trained field systems users.
Created invoice-reconciliation program that resulted in capturing an average of $5,000 per month in vendor overcharges.

Systems Analyst, Computer Services Organization, June 1992 to June 1994
Designed and implemented systems for crude-oil acquisition applications.
Performed system maintenance programming.
Wrote computer system procedure specifications and user manuals.
Designed and supervised programming of tracking system that determined more cost-effective transportation routes.

Systems Proficiency
Hardware: IBM 3090, MVS Operating System/JES2, IBM PS/2 Model 55
Programming Languages: NATURAL/ADABAS, JCL, SAR, SAS, FOCUS, QMF/SQL with DB2, UCC7, ROSCOE, TSO, ISPF, Predict, COBOL, BASIC, PL/1, IBM ASSEMBLER
PC Software: DBase III+, LOTUS Release 3, Harvard Graphics, LOTUS Freelance Plus, DOS, PCTools, PC Focus

Education
1992   B.S., Business Administration/Management Information Systems
Bowling Green State University, Bowling Green, Ohio, 3.7/4.0 GPA

Violating the Traditional Rule of Brevity

Different Readers Will Read Different Parts

This resume violates all the traditional rules of brevity and usually prompts the initial response: "No one will read all this!"

"That's correct," says Michael Kenney, president of KCDM Associates, consultants in organizational and individual transition. "No one will read *all* of the resume, but different readers will read different parts."

Kenney points out that resumes have two readers: screeners, who are narrowing the applicant pool to the most appropriate candidates, and decision makers, who actually make hiring decisions.

"Most rules concerning resumes have been formulated to make them appealing to screeners," Kenney adds. "This is particularly true if you perceive the most common way to reach a decision maker is through a recruiter or human resource department. Actually, less than 50 percent of all job offers are created this way."

Screeners make decisions based on job specifications they have been given, which are invariably couched in terms of credentials and experience. The first two pages of Robert Letterman's resume address those issues.

Decision makers make hiring decisions based on such issues as the candidate's style and fit, his or her skills and past contributions or problem-solving experience. The last two pages of Robert's resume address those concerns directly.

"Complaints about the length of this resume come from screeners who, after all, don't need all this information," explains Kenney. "For that reason, there are occasions when I might suggest that a candidate simply send the first two pages in the mail. However, most of the compliments come from CEOs and COOs—those who would actually hire someone like Robert—because the full resume provides more information than a simple, chronological resume. For that reason, I urge that candidates provide the line manager with the four-page format before or during the interview process."

Incidentally, Robert was able to continue his career in the health care industry as a human resources professional, despite a tight market and downsizing. This resume is actually printed on 11" x 17" paper stock and folded in the middle to avoid losing pages.

Michael J. Kenney
President, KCDM Associates

Michael J. Kenney, president of KCDM Associates, has spent the last quarter century of his professional life dealing with career-related issues, including outplacement services and individual career counseling. He also consults with companies establishing internal career development programs for their existing workforces and works with human resource professionals primarily in selection issues.

Based in Indianapolis, Ind., KCDM is a human resource consulting firm that provides outplacement services as well as management and organizational development consultation to a wide variety of client companies and nonprofit organizations.

ROBERT LETTERMAN
902 North Meridian Street, #250
Indianapolis, IN 46204
(317) 643-4234

OBJECTIVE: An executive human resource position in an entrepreneurial, growing organization that is value driven and has the vision to appreciate that its success is a by-product of its respect and commitment to its human assets. The position would ideally require participation in the overall direction of the corporation and its involvement in major decisions from the human resource management perspective.

EDUCATION: M.B.A., University of Dayton, Marketing and Economics, 1968.
B.A., University of Dayton, Spanish and Philosophy, 1965.

EXPERIENCE: **ST. VINCENT HOSPITAL AND HEALTHCARE CENTER, INC.,** Indianapolis, Indiana.
August 1987 VICE-PRESIDENT, HUMAN RESOURCES
to
July 1988 Managed a multi-site human resource function of 19 employees in a tertiary care medical center comprised of 800 beds and 4,000 employees. Coordinated the development of a succession planning process; negotiated a significant increase in computer hardware capacity with no increase in cost; coordinated the development of a gainsharing process for all employees; shifted emphasis of wage and salary program from an internal equity basis to a market position basis.

Major Accomplishment: Initiated the development of a multi-purpose childcare center to house 200 children, provide pre-and afterschool care, a sick child drop-off program and a summer day service. Accomplished this task by joining independent corporations in a joint venture. Childcare center is scheduled to open in September 1988. Was able to accomplish this task with no budget allocation.

September 1982 **McLEAN HOSPITAL,** Belmont, Massachusetts.
to ASSISTANT DIRECTOR FOR HOSPITAL SERVICES (2/86 to 8/87)
August 1987

Provide guidance, vision and support for a number of departments, including Human Resources, Building Services, Safety, Security, Nutrition Services, Telecommunication Services. Printing Services and Mail Delivery/Transport Services at this world renowned, Harvard affiliated psychiatric teaching / research hospital comprised of 2,200 employees. Introduced a new patient feeding system; upgraded the print shop resulting in 95% of all jobs being done in-house and annual savings of $60,000; created a separate safety department; renegotiated the call-pager system resulting in a significant upgrade at a savings of $8,000 per year.

Major Accomplishment: Developed a mail and supplies transport system to cover 42 buildings and 240 acres resulting in many operating efficiencies and a labor savings of approximately $91,000 annually.

ASSISTANT DIRECTOR FOR HUMAN RESOURCES (9/82 to 2/86)

Managed a staff of 18 persons involved in all areas of human resource management. Reduced human resource operating budget of $600,000; coordinated the development of an on-site childcare center; created an eight page quarterly human resource newsletter; revamped employee appeal procedure, created and organized the McLean Hospital Walk and Run for Mental Health.

Major Accomplishment: Planned, designed and implemented the total reorganization of the Human Resource function without changes in manpower complement. Created new functions including Human Resource Development, Employee Relations, Internal Communications and Human Resource Information Systems.

August 1979
to
September 1982

CARNEY HOSPITAL, Boston Massachusetts.
VICE-PRESIDENT, HUMAN RESOURCES

Provided division support and guidance for a staff of nineteen people in a 400 bed community / teaching hospital with 2,000 employees. Established a nurse and allied health registry with three other hospitals; renegotiated life and health insurance policies with first year saving of $24,000 and $75,000 respectively; establish a human relations function; removed ten CRNA's and twenty head nurses from bargaining unit; spearheaded corporate move to self-insure Worker's Compensation at an annual savings of $300,000.

Major Accomplishment: Developed a separate off-site education and conference center to satisfy hospital training needs, sell programs and space to the healthcare community at large and enhance the hospital's image as a teaching institution. Center was able to be financially solvent within its first year of operation.

September 1975
to
August 1979

ST. MARGARET HOSPITAL, Hammond, Indiana.
DIRECTOR, EMPLOYEE RELATIONS

Directed an eleven human resource function in a 475 bed tertiary care community hospital with 1,500 employees. Reduced turnover from 29.8% to 10%; spearheaded corporate consolidation of life, LTD and STD plans resulting in annual savings of $250,000; reactivated job bidding system; redeveloped a two shift human resource function.

Major Accomplishment: Totally revamped suggestion system resulting in 900 suggestions per year, 30% acceptance and implementation rate and recipient of NASS Outstanding Performance Award for three consecutive years (first hospital ever to receive this award).

November 1971
to
September 1975

ST. JOSEPH MEMORIAL HOSPITAL, Kokomo, Indiana.
PERSONNEL DIRECTOR

Managed a six person personnel function in a 250 bed community hospital with 750 employees. Established a formal health service; developed a supervisory training program and discussion group; together with Safety Director, initiated various safety programs.

Major Accomplishment: Automated all personnel data and created a variety of management reports such as labor variance, turnover, position control and manpower planning.

April 1969
to
November 1971

RCA CORPORATION, Indianapolis, Indiana.
SALARIED RECRUITER, RETIREMENT PLAN ADMINISTRATOR, PDS COORDINATOR

Performed the functions associated with the above mentioned titles for two operating divisions comprised of 1,200 employees.

June 1968
to
April 1969

PHILCO-FORD CORPORATION, Connersville, Indiana.
SENIOR EMPLOYMENT REPRESENTATIVE

Recruited, selected, conducted exit interviews and coordinated new employee follow-up program for this 6,800 employee operating division; also prepared manpower reports and wrote job descriptions.

May 1967
to
June 1968

DEFENSE ELECTRONICS SUPPLY CENTER, Dayton, Ohio.
PROCUREMENT AGENT

Solicited vendors, evaluated bids, read blueprints and awarded contracts in accordance with ASPR while completing M.B.A. on a full-time basis.

May 1966
to
May 1967

UNIVERSITY OF DAYTON, Dayton, Ohio.
ADMISSIONS COUNSELOR

Traveled throughout the United States recruiting high school students for the university.

SIGNIFICANT ACCOMPLISHMENTS

COST EFFECTIVENESS:

The ability to preserve or expand service or products while reducing cost.
- Renegotiated life and health policies at an annual savings of $24,000 and $75,000, respectively.
- Spearheaded corporate effort to self-insure Worker's Compensation at a per annum savings of $250,000.
- Reduced human resource budget by $600,000.
- Reduced attorney's fees by $200,000.
- Upgraded print shop operations resulting in $600,000 a year savings.
- Renegotiated call-pager system at a savings of $8,000 per year.

CREATIVE LEADERSHIP:

The ability to find new ways to do things through others.
- Created the McLean Hospital Walk and Run for Mental Health.
- Created and staffed an off-site education and conference center.
- Reduced turnover from 29.8% to 10%.
- Negotiated the withdrawal of ten RNA's and twenty head nurses from bargaining unit.
- Created a human relations function.
- Orchestrated a joint venture to create a childcare center.
- Developed, with three other hospitals, a nurse registry.

SYSTEMS INNOVATION:

The ability to create new models to provide better services.
- Developed an automated human resource information system
- Revised human resource organization resulting in several new functions.
- Created a two shift human resource organization.
- Created a new division entitled Institutional Advancement.
- Created a mail delivery / supplies transport service.

PROGRAM DEVELOPMENT:

The ability to create new programs and/or model existing programs.
- Created a human resources quarterly newsletter.
- Revised employee appeal procedure to a mediation model.
- Reformatted employee handbook.
- Instituted a large number of "no cost" benefits.
- Negotiated with bank to provide on-campus ATM services, direct deposit and free checking services.

PROFESSIONAL AND CIVIC AFFILIATIONS:

Past President, Indiana Society for Healthcare Human Resource Administration
Member, Massachusetts Big Brothers, Board of Directors
Vice-Chairman, Massachusetts Bay Area United Way Campaign, Medical Division
Member, Calumet Area United Health Service, Inc., Board of Directors
Member, various human resource organizations.

REMARKS:

I am a focused, self-disciplined person who is able to see an opportunity, define a goal, and develop a plan to achieve it. Whether it is developing a plan to lose weight (I lost seventy pounds in one year) or becoming an accomplished long distance runner (I qualified and ran in the last five Boston Marathons), I am able to be realistic about my abilities to achieve results. I am a collaborative person and feel most comfortable working with a group and being part of a team. I enjoy taking on challenges and I have been told by many people that they appreciate the authenticity, sense of humor and enthusiasm I bring to each activity I encounter. I am situational rather than dogmatic in approaching judgmental situations and I bring patience and flexibility to play in the advice I give and the decisions I make.

AREAS OF EFFECTIVENESS

INNOVATIVE AND EFFECTIVE DESIGNER

McLean Hospital had for many years been interested in developing childcare services but had not done so. I envisioned the possibility of a childcare center, researched its history at McLean, gathered key people together, formed a plan, and assigned task forces to investigate key aspects of the plan. We concluded that we wanted an on-site facility designed for children, a full service program, and a parent-dominated non-profit corporate organization. I was able to divert $200,000 from existing funds under my jurisdiction and build a facility using hospital skilled trades people. The resultant childcare center not only met a long standing need, but gave employees a sense of empowerment and faith in the organization which had been absent.

The Carney Hospital needed to provide training and skills building programs at every organization level. I saw this issue not only as a problem, but as an opportunity to increase the hospital's visibility in the community and have a greater influence on the local healthcare delivery structure. I convinced hospital management that we should have a separate education and conference center and that the center could be self-sufficient. I was able to centralize all hospital training resources in my division, hired a Director of Training and Development, and found an off-site facility. We remodeled the facility, developed an education curriculum, and opened the center with a staff of thirteen people. The Center became totally self-sufficient in the first year, the hospital gained access to previously unavailable programs and facilities, and the center became a symbol of the progressive cutting edge leadership of the hospital.

OPPORTUNISTIC INITIATOR

St. Margaret Hospital had a history of employee unrest which at one point resulted in a wildcat strike. The organization had a number of problems centered around a lack of communication and empowerment. Although the hospital. had a suggestion plan it was terribly under utilized. I worked with the Coordinator of Suggestion Systems to revise the plan, to provide greater financial incentives, greater employee and supervisor recognition, and timely and thorough evaluation of suggestions. The result was that in the first year 900 suggestions were submitted and more than 30% were awarded and implemented. The result was that the Plan became an effective and positive communication vehicle, employees felt respected and empowered, and for the next three years the Plan received the Outstanding Performance Award of the National Association of Suggestion Systems. This award had previously never been given by NASS to a hospital.

The Carney Hospital was located in a very old, traditional, blue collar, Irish neighborhood In South Boston, which was undergoing a racial mix transition. The hospital needed to demonstrate its willingness to serve and employ the new minority groups moving in the area. The changes occurring in the hospital and the community were producing racial tensions and threatening the harmony of the hospital setting. I saw this situation as an opportunity to increase organization awareness about minority groups and to take a leadership role in the community that would develop the alliances necessary for us to expand our patient base. I developed a proposal for a human relations function reporting to the Executive Vice-President/CEO. Although my proposal was approved, I was asked to have the function report to me. I accepted that compromise, hired a Director of Human Relations and established the function. Four months later, I renegotiated the position to report to the Executive Vice-President. The result was that the Director of Human Relations was able to develop a new position atmosphere concerning minority relations at the hospital and was able to open many community doors which had hitherto been closed.

FACILITATIVE COACH

The Human Resource function at McLean Hospital had little credibility and was under utilized. Although staff members had many skills, they possessed low self and group esteem. I worked closely with them to identify their skills, various organization issues, and the solutions necessary to make things better. The result was that we created a number of new functions including Human Resource Development, Internal Communications, Employee Relations, and Human Resource Automated Information Systems, without adding staff or increasing our budget complement. Our new sense of pride and confidence helped us portray a positive "can do" image and we gained new organizational respect and credibility.

McLean Hospital resides on a 240 acre campus with 42 buildings and 21 locked mental health patient units. I was interested in finding a way to get the entire organization involved in a meaningful group activity that would foster organization pride, and give people from diverse professional backgrounds the opportunity to work together. I proposed that we stage a major road race with the proceeds going to mental health research. After gaining approval and $5,000 of seed money, I gathered together individuals who I believed would be helpful. Together we devised a plan, issued assignments and formed task forces. I directed the group and guided them through the process. The result was that more than 200 employees volunteered and hundreds of others participated as walkers and runners. The McLean Hospital Walk and Run for Mental Health annually has more than 800 participants and to date has raised more then $15,000.

Power Resume Tip

Include information about your high school education only if you are a recent graduate or did not attend college or a trade school—in other words, if it is the most important educational credential you have.

Lights, Camera, Action (Verbs)!

Exciting the Potential Employer

"This resume emphasizes what the individual can do for the company, not what the company can do for the individual," according to Sharon Worlton and Sally Morrison of LDS Employment in Naperville, Ill. "That's one of the reasons it is one of our favorites."

Other reasons high on Worlton and Morrison's list include:

- It is clean with lots of white space.
- It uses short, concise statements, making it easy to read quickly.
- It begins selling the individual in the very first sentence and then it *sells, sells, sells*.
- It focuses on achievements using specific numbers, percents and money.
- It uses action verbs to start off each accomplishment.
- If the double lines were eliminated at the top, it would be computer scannable.
- It uses key words that a human resources person would be seeking.
- Overall impression: professional, brief and capable.

Sharon Worlton and Sally Morrison
LDS Employment

Sharon Worlton and Sally Morrison are employees of LDS Employment, a nonprofit organization supported by the Church of Jesus Christ of Latter-Day Saints. They work with individuals from a very wide range of professions (from general labor to CEOs). Their program provides job search training, job and network referrals, career counseling, resume assistance and a job seeker's resource center with telephones, fax service, typewriters and computers. All services are free. Sharon has worked for LDS Employment for 10 years, and Sally has worked there for seven. Sharon just completed serving as past president of the National Association for Job Search Training.

NANCY L. CRENSHAW
000 West Hollywood
Los Angeles, California 90022
(111) 992-0001 Home
(111) 886-1236 Messages

Experienced human resource professional with strong interpersonal, communication and organizational skills. Achievement recognized in the design and implementation of innovative, cost-effective programs in communications, benefits and employee relations.

EXPERIENCE

Armour Dial Corporation, Downers Grove, IL., 1989 to Present

Benefit Analyst
- Restyled company-wide newsletter to a more positive employee-oriented communication tool. 1991 cost for bi-monthly publication for 12,000 employees was $ 52,000.00.
- Authored 90% of all employee and ERISA-mandated communications and reports such as summary-plan descriptions, employee handbook and revisions, and 5,500 filings and summary-annual reports.
- Restructured corporate short-term disability program to incorporate third-party medical review. Savings for first year were $50,000.
- Designed and installed a direct certification system with insurance carriers. System eliminated extension of benefits to ineligibles.

McDonald's Corporation, Oak Brook, IL., 1977 to 1989

Benefit Analyst, 1984-1989
- Spearheaded contagious disease task force to control in-store instances of infectious disease; instrumental in preventing store shutdowns.
- Acted as trouble-shooter on short-term and long-term disability claims, sought medical review where necessary and resolved claim disputes.
- Responsible for indemnity and HMO plan administration including communications and enrollment for 15,000 employees nationwide.
- Monitored flexible-spending account, pre-tax dependent care program for Company: ensured success for maintenance of program. Proposed elimination due to administration expense and low employee participation.

Relocation Specialist, 1977-1984
- Managed all phases of in-house executive relocation program. This entailed appraisal process, equity advances, final-closing documentation and home inventory negotiations. Relocated 220 executives per year.

EDUCATION & DESIGNATIONS

City College. 3.67 GPA (9 courses remaining for BA, English)
Chairman, New England Village Homeowner Association

A Resume with Personality

This Candidate Went Out On a Limb Without Falling

"This resume defies convention in several ways," says Cathy Kennedy, vice president of Lee Hecht Harrison, one of the nation's largest and most well-known outplacement firms.

"Although the writer has at least 26 years of experience, he has covered everything in one page. That's certainly not the norm, but it is very important for someone in the advertising business who communicates with words!"

Kennedy also notes that George Smith's resume is unusual because of the many things it *doesn't* have. Notice that Smith omitted dates of employment and a job objective. "By not using dates," says Kennedy, "the writer has lessened the possible temptation for the resume reviewer to judge him first by his age. And by not including a job objective, the candidate keeps the door wide open for opportunities on either the agency or client side of the business."

Also notice that the candidate has shunned the usual "resume speak"—incomplete sentences, phrases beginning with action words—in favor of a "story" in the first person. The result is that this document sounds less like a resume than it does a conversation with a person you meet at a party.

"This resume has personality," emphasizes Kennedy. "From the 12-word summary statement at the top—which tells the reader succinctly what the writer is all about—to the organization of the document, to the breezy yet highly professional style, the resume works!"

Cathy Kennedy
Vice President, Lee Hecht Harrison

Lee Hecht Harrison is an international premier outplacement and career management firm, with offices located throughout the United States, Europe and Australia. Founded in 1974, the company helps organizations and their employees deal with today's complex and challenging career transition issues.

George L. Smith

531 Church Street
New York, NY 10044

Office: 212-555-2000
Home: 212-555-6180

A major advertising agency account executive who used to be a client.

MY BACKGROUND

Ad Agency DDB Needham. Account Supervisor in this agency and its great predecessor, Doyle Dane Bernbach, for over 12 years. The account is GTE. Primarily, I have worked in the corporate account areas. Additionally, I have handled GTE defense systems, precious metals, electrical and electronic equipment and commercial/industrial lighting.

In a nutshell, it's my job to draw out pertinent marketing/product/service information and relay it to appropriate people in the agency. Then, to represent the agency in presenting the resulting work to the client.

I've worked with all media including network TV, business and consumer magazines, outdoor, radio and newspapers. And, of course, I work on a daily basis with clients, agency management, creatives and media representatives.

Client Sylvania Electrical Products. For 14 years, I was with this major electronics corporation. I worked in all areas of sales promotion, advertising and other activities, serving several divisions as Ad Manager and/or Marketing Services Manager. I had to interface effectively with company management, suppliers, distributors, retailers and the advertising agency.

ABOUT ME

St. Johns University and Queens College—Marketing.
Willing to relocate (though I love New York, too).
Excellent health, married.

A Resume That Grabs and Keeps On Grabbing

Clear Layout Focuses on Accomplishments

The generous amounts of white space and the boldface type grabbed Claudia A. Gentner, chief information officer for Lee Hecht Harrison, when she first looked at it.

"I immediately understood that this candidate was a planning executive at the vice president level," said the career consultant. "All of that happened in a moment."

"In the next instant," she continued, "the reader can *absorb* the writer's experience in three management chunks, giving the impression of stability and commitment to organization. If the reader still has interest, in the next moment, company names become evident."

Then the reader gets to the "real content" of the resume—the accomplishment statements.

Gentner praises the elegance of this resume. She points to the summary at the top. "My preference is for a brief summary statement that doubles as an objective. Note the use of the term Planning Executive. What does this person do? Succinctly: 'Formulate business objectives and develop plans to achieve them.' That's elegantly stated. Just enough words to explain the focus of the candidate's job function."

Gentner also states that those who know this candidate or who read his resume closely "recognize he's a transportation planning executive. But his planning skills are certainly transferable to other contexts and his intention here is to appeal to a broader readership than the transportation industry."

Claudia A. Gentner
Chief Information Officer, Lee Hecht Harrison

Before assuming responsibilities as chief information officer for Lee Hecht Harrison, one of the nation's premier outplacement firms, Claudia Gentner co-founded and served as senior vice president of Seagate Associates, a New Jersey-based career transition consulting firm, now a Lee Hecht Harrison company. Gentner established Seagate's Business Information Center, which is the first such facility in the outplacement industry dedicated to the information needs of job seekers. She is a frequent contributor to leading human resources publications and is listed in *Who's Who in Finance and Industry*.

PLANNING EXECUTIVE

Formulate business objectives and develop plans to achieve them.

1988-present   **Vice President, Resource Planning**
Purolator Courier Corp., Basking Ridge, N.J.

Through a staff of 60, direct all planning activities for the U.S. Courier Division's transportation network, facilities, equipment, purchasing and procurement.

Creating the company's first formal tactical and strategic operations-oriented planning group.

Developed and managed the capital budget for expenditures averaging $57+ million per year.

Selected Indianapolis as the firm's air service hub. Negotiated the site development contracts and directed the facilities construction program.

Developed aircraft fleet plans and schedules. Directed the acquisition of a fleet of large turbo-prop and heavy jet aircraft. Negotiated long-term aircraft operating agreements with independent contractors.

Designed and implemented a plan to eliminate excess motor vehicle capacity through a sale and the leaseback of fewer, more fuel-efficient vehicles. Annual cost savings of $6.1 million.

1983-1988   **Vice President**
Simat, Helliesen and Eichner, Inc., New York, N.Y.

Senior project director for a firm of transportation industry economists and planners who provide consulting services to companies involved in transportation.

Created complete business, organizational, operational and financial plans for air and ground carriers.

Directed strategic and tactical planning projects involving market and marketing studies, cost and pricing models, forecasting, route and fleet planning, flight equipment and capital investment evaluations.

Prepared diversification studies and economic analyses of potential mergers.

Developed strategies, evidence and testimony in antitrust litigations and labor arbitration proceedings.

1970-1983   **Senior Director, Passenger Pricing**
                 Director, Freight Pricing
                 American Airlines, Inc., New York, N.Y.

Formulated and implemented profitable and innovative passenger, freight, mail and express pricing policies with supporting regulatory, marketing and operational strategies.

Instituted several cost-related system passenger fare changes, including the precedent-setting "Super Saver" program, that increased annual revenues $103+ million.

Created the company's strategic position, with all economic supporting evidence, for the CAB's investigation of all U.S. carriers' pricing policies and rate levels.

Served as the company's representative on passenger and cargo-related matters to the International Air Transportation Association and the Air Transportation Association of America.

EDUCATION

BA Political Science, 1970
Providence College

Graduate work in Law and Business (36 credits), 1970-1972
St. John's University Law School

Power Resume Tip

Use single spacing for individual listings and double spacing between sections and paragraphs. This divides information into easily digestible doses and wards off the "sea of type" look, which is intimidating and difficult to read.

Short On Words, Long On Accomplishments

Getting to the Heart of the Matter

Reading this resume, one definitely gets the impression that this candidate can sell, sell, sell. The recognition she's received from her two most recent employers jumps off the page to a hiring manager looking for a sales person who can really produce.

Ellen Lerner, Certified Personnel Consultant, was attracted to this resume because of its "successful melding of several resume formats" including chronological and functional. Lerner notes that this resume "leaves the reader with a clear picture of the candidate's accomplishments and skills."

"There are not extra words, paragraphs or descriptive sentences," notes Lerner. "Bold type and ample white space are used to direct the reader's eye."

Lerner also appreciated that this candidate featured her accomplishments by using bullets. In addition, "nothing is repeated and irrelevant. Interesting, earlier experience is downplayed, but nonetheless provided in abbreviated form."

Lynn Levy's brief explanation of the hiatus in her career from 1974 to 1985 is one that employers will immediately understand. Had she been involved in volunteer activities during that time, she might have chosen to highlight some of her accomplishments during that period. But as Lerner notes, "it's best to leave out information that does not help convince employers that you're the best candidate for the job."

"Even after only a brief scanning of this resume, the reader is left with a positive impression that this candidate is indeed a winner."

Ellen Lerner, CPC

Ellen Lerner, Certified Personnel Consultant, is a writer, trainer and former president of Lerner International, Md. Before starting her own company in July 1990, she was the director of the hotel division for Roth Young Personnel.

Lerner International was the only executive recruitment firm considered a specialist in professional meeting planning and hotel sales and marketing industries.

An accomplished writer, Lerner has had articles published in *The Meeting Manager* and a variety of association newsletters. She presently writes a regularly featured career column for *Meetings & Conventions*.

Committed to shifting people's orientation from *crisis management* to *professional career management*, she has written and delivered the master career series nationally.

LYNN LEVY
25 Mayflower Court
Westminster, MD 21208
410-555-4849

Employment
==========

2/89-1/96   **SALES REPRESENTATIVE**—TRIA, New York, NY
(The Research Institute of America)

- 1991—Member, Most Improved Region
- 1992—Member, Region of the Year
- 1993—National Representative of the Month
- 1989-1995—Winner of every incentive contest

Sold professional libraries to accountants, lawyers and corporations in the fields of tax, estate planning, real estate, pensions, benefits, employment and discrimination. Territory included Baltimore City (south to Crofton, Md.).

1985-1989   **SALES MANAGER**—Cooper Dental Laboratory, Baltimore, Md.

- 1986-1988—#1 sales representative in company
- 1987—Promoted to manager

   *   Initiated outside sales   *   Telemarketing
   *   Newsletter production   *   Client liaison
   *   Client seminars   *   Wrote marketing plan
   *   Direct mail

1974-1985   Family responsibilities

1970-1974   Group Therapist at North Charles General Hospital
Vice President, V.M. Real Estate, Inc.
Social Worker for the Department of Social Services, Baltimore and
    Cook County Hospital, Chicago.

Education
=========

1970   B.A. Sociology, University of Maryland

A Good Presentation Despite
Lack of Experience

A Demonstration of Commitment and Interests

Perhaps those candidates who have the most difficulty writing their resumes are candidates who don't yet have on-the-job experience.

Faced with this dilemma, Sam Jones, the candidate whose resume appears on the opposite page, chose not to "snow" prospective employers, as so many candidates in his position do. Instead, he "highlights his education, the skills relating to his area of interest, related work experience and special information on awards," points out Susan M. Gordon. She is president of Lynne Palmer Executive Recruitment, Inc., a New York-based firm specializing in the communications field.

Knowing full well that in publishing he would probably have to launch his career in a clerical position, Jones chose not to include an Objective, which undoubtedly would have appeared presumptuous.

Instead, this resume, "clearly positions his areas of interest in graphic arts and design," says Gordon. "His internship suggests that he is ambitious and hardworking. And his education background at prestigious schools, along with two excellent awards, suggests that he has a great deal of talent."

Susan M. Gordon
Lynne Palmer Executive Recruitment, Inc.
Lynne Palmer Executive Recruitment, Inc., is a personnel recruiting firm specializing in the communications area—books and magazines. The company was established in 1964 and serves the publishing industry nationwide on all levels (entry-level to executive).

SAM JONES

123 Amber Street
Jefferson City, Missouri 65107

EDUCATION

B.A. French Language & Literature
Photography
University of Missouri, May 1997
University of Paris, Sorbonne 1995-1996

SKILLS

Desktop publishing—Quark XPress and Pagemaker
Photography—B & W and Color darkroom knowledge

SELECTED WORK
EXPERIENCE

10/96 - Present

ABC Magazine—Production Intern
Trafficking ads through various stages
Clerical Assistant to V.P., Production
Work with desktop publishing system

9/95 - 5/96

University of Missouri, School of Art
Responsible for aiding students with use of software for
graphic design class

AWARDS & PUBLICATIONS

Finalist, 1997 Photography Award
Tom Jay Award, 1996, for Photography

LANGUAGES

French, Italian

A Long List In a Little Space

"King of the One-Liners"

The most impressive thing about Peter Blue's resume is that it says so much in a relatively small amount of space. It does this by allotting one line, and one line only, to each of a long list of accomplishments.

"Writing one-line thoughts requires great discipline and really enforces economy of language, but it has great impact on the reader," says Howard Bennett, vice president, outplacement for Power Marketing, a San Francisco-based outplacement firm.

Bennett notes that Blue's resume is a good illustration of some other basic resume rules he advises:

1. Use the chronological format. *Never* write a functional resume—headhunters and corporate employment managers regard them as "problem" resumes and are suspicious of candidates who use them.

2. One, two and even three page resumes are okay, depending upon your background and length of tenure. If you have 10 or more years of significant achievements, don't shortchange yourself by trying to stick to one page. Just be sure to sell yourself on the first page.

3. Put a clear, targeted objective at the top—the very best kind is a job title or professional title. Then support the objective with a brief qualifications summary that features your important selling points.

4. When writing about your experience, *quantify everything*. Give names, numbers and definitions—all of these add to your credibility.

5. Don't miss the opportunity to demonstrate promotions within an organization.

6. Demonstrate your skills by telling stories—describe major projects that showcase your talents and separate you from the competition. Be sure to list bottom-line achievements.

7. Leave lots of white space and use bullets, underlining and bold type for emphasis, but don't overdo graphics. Employ nonjustified type and "gaze motion" (smooth curves on the right margin of paragraphs) so that the eye moves comfortably down the page.

Howard Bennett
Vice President, Outplacement, Power Marketing

Power Marketing, a San Francisco-based corporate outplacement firm, has brought a pragmatic, marketing-based approach to the job search. Power Marketing uses the same brand management techniques in the job market that Procter & Gamble uses to sell consumer products. Its methods have achieved results (in the form of new jobs) for candidates ranging from plant workers to $1 million-a-year CEOs.

PETER BLUE
1234 56th Avenue
San Francisco, CA 94567
415-555-4567

MANAGER OF LOGISTICS & DISTRIBUTION

QUALIFICATIONS   BBA-Personnel Management, 20 years in distribution management
Specialist in work and manpower planning and quality improvement
Experience in inventory control software development and application
Background in hazardous materials storage, transportation, disposal

---

PROFESSIONAL EXPERIENCE

ABC Scientific, Inc., Colma, CA   1990 to Present
REGIONAL WAREHOUSE MANAGER

Manage warehouse for $600 million international scientific products distributor.
Responsible for western region including California, Washington and Pacific Rim. Administer $3.2MM operating budget, report to Regional Distribution Manager.
Direct six supervisors, 60 union warehousepersons and six support staff.

Responsible for $13MM inventory, 80,000 line items, 230,000 sq. ft. warehouse.
Manage receiving, checking, picking, packing and shipping of 1,500 orders daily.
Operate facility in compliance with OSHA and DOT standards.

Distribute scientific, laboratory, photographic supplies and equipment.
Products and equipment include chemicals, hazardous materials, lab furniture, diagnostic instruments, cleanroom and lab supplies, refrigerated and sterile items.

Serve clients in education, biotechnology, soil testing and water treatment industries including Syntex, UCSF, UCLA, Stanford, Kodak, Amgen, IBM, CH2M Hill.
Work with 900 manufacturers including Nalge, Corning Glass, JT Baker, EM Science.

Major Projects

Established procedures for hazardous material storage and disposal.
Developed and implemented hazardous material stock rotation plan.
Conducted hazardous material/safety training for employees.

Developed and implemented performance and quality improvement program.
Redefined warehouse positions, established hourly production standards.

Streamlined inventory identification and tracking system.
Introduced systematic analysis of daily discrepancy reports.
Standardized receiving, stocking, checking and housekeeping procedures.

Achievements
* Saved 10% in packing costs by recycling and use of alternative packing materials.
* Reduced inventory discrepancies 45% annually by developing tracking system.
* Cut disposal of hazardous materials 50% by implementing storage procedures.
* Increased employee productivity 15% by establishing production standards.
* Reduced injury claims 40% by introducing safety awareness program.
* Consistently met 24-hour turnaround goal for 93% of shipments.
* Reduced breakage 80% by designing new product packaging.

Continued....

PROFESSIONAL EXPERIENCE (Continued)

XYZ Tire Company, Chicago/Reno   1973 to 1990
DISTRIBUTION MANAGER (1988 to 1990)

Managed 425,000 sq. ft. warehouse for $2 billion rubber products manufacturer.
Responsible for $15MM, 500,000-unit tire inventory and public warehouse operation.
Supervised 10 administrative staff, directed 45 contract warehousepersons.
Managed $2MM budget, reported to National Distribution Manager.

Supervised receiving, inventory control, storage, security, distribution, traffic.
Scheduled drivers, negotiated rates and routes with truck lines/carriers.

Managed product distribution, security and receivables for 24 public accounts.
Inventory included appliances, chemicals, hospital supplies, electronic products.

Major Projects/Achievements
* Increased productivity 10% by application of WOFAC-based computerized systems.
* Increased storage capacity 10% by standardizing inventory control procedures.
* Developed operations manual and cross-training plan for six job functions.
* Upgraded warehouse output from lowest in company ranking to second.
* Implemented special security procedures for public accountants.

ASSISTANT DISTRIBUTION MANAGER (1979 to 1988)

Responsible for warehouse administration of 200,000 sq. ft. facility.
Received and shipped 20,000 tires daily to 11 western states and Pacific Rim.
Managed receiving, storage and shipping of $7 million tire inventory.
Supervised 50 warehousepersons and data processing staff.

Major Projects/Achievements
* Increased productivity over 15% through WOFAC work measurement program.
* Consulted to four regional facilities to improve manpower planning.
* Designed and wrote audit approved cycle inventory procedures.
* Established personnel policies and procedures.

WAREHOUSE SUPERVISOR (1977 to 1979)

Supervised 100,000 sq. ft. facility with $5 million inventory.
Inventory included tires, footwear, industrial products, auto/home supplies.

WAREHOUSE FOREMAN (1973 to 1977)

Responsible for receiving, storage, shipping, order entry and customer service.
Supervised 22 union warehousepersons and 16 support staff.

* Joined company as Order Entry Clerk; promoted to Foreman after two years.

EDUCATION	BBA, Personnel Management, Northwestern University, Chicago, 1980 Completed 15 MBA units, University of Nevada, Las Vegas, 1988
PROFESSIONAL	Completed courses/seminars in hazardous waste, transportation, traffic, safety, employee involvement and leadership
TECHNICAL	IBM Mainframe, DEC 1050, BASIC

Power Resume Tip

When amateurs mix typefaces, the results are usually not impressive. It's best to choose a typeface and stick with it, leaving the mixing of fonts to trained graphic artists.

Don't Make the Reader Dig for the Gem

Working with a Gold Mine of Experience

"Bill Sullivan is a highly accomplished person whose initial resume gave virtually no indication of the depth and breadth of his experience and accomplishments," explains Mark Freedman, managing director of The Resource Planning Group (RPG) of Rye, N.Y. "He wanted to move on to more challenging duties in a larger company."

The challenge, says Freedman (who launched Executive Career Strategies, a division of RPG), was to take what existed and mold the material into a more formidable presentation.

"Visually, it was disastrous," he explains. "There were unremittingly dense blocks of print that discouraged even the most fearless reader from trying to dig out the gems, if they could be found. The font size was too small, and most tellingly, the opening summary was a boring laundry list with no indication of the real strengths that would show why Bill would be an ideal candidate for the position he sought."

After one or two run-throughs, neither Bill nor Freedman were satisfied. The resume contained all of the information, but it was still flat.

"I was sure there had to be more to Bill than what he'd presented," says the consultant. "We just started talking on the phone one evening, and I let the conversation flow. The next thing I knew, Bill was excitingly describing a major accomplishment that I'd not heard before."

What resulted was a more concise idea of just how comprehensive and vital some of Bill's key achievements were. Freedman was able to craft the resume to be more visually appealing, using white space to showcase Bill's achievements and reflect the unique qualities that make him a top candidate in his field.

"These moments of relaxed conversation with my clients have repeatedly yielded gold mines of quality information that make the person a more compelling candidate," Freedman adds.

Mark S. Freedman
Managing Director, The Resource Planning Group

Mark Freedman is managing director of The Resource Planning Group (RPG), a human resources consulting firm which assists individuals and companies manage change. He launched Executive Career Strategies (ECS), a division of RPG, in 1994. ECS provides research, cover letter and resume development and production.

In addition, Freedman has alliances with national job banks to provide resume consultation and development to their memberships. He also has served as a consultant to several *Fortune 100* companies, assisting them with the application of computer technology to human resource initiatives, including compensation, succession planning and training.

He is skilled in computer graphics and design and applies that knowledge in both consulting assignments and resume production.

William Sullivan

45 Martindale Drive   423-887-9643 [H]
Chattanooga, Tennessee 37447   423-887-8458 [Fax]

SENIOR INTERNATIONAL HUMAN RESOURCES EXECUTIVE
High-impact - Merge & Manage Seamless Multi-cultural/Multi-national Operations

---

Domestic and international Human Resources businessperson with extensive experience in multi-plant, offshore and start-up environments. A dedicated, market-driven manager capable of joining nine culturally diverse subsidiaries on three continents into one HR function, while maintaining cultural identity and profitable operations. An architect of motivated, productive teams that have positive bottom line impact. Innovative, entrepreneurial, and pragmatic problem-solver efficient at building a progressive partnership with management to maximize resources and value. Expertise in:

- Organizational Design
- Mergers/Acquisitions
- Management Development
- Training
- Compensation/Benefits

- Union Avoidance
- Policy Development/Administration
- Succession Planning
- Quality Initiatives (QS-9000)
- Strategic Planning

PROFESSIONAL EXPERIENCE

CARDIFF TECHNOLOGIES, INC., Chattanooga, TN   1988 - Present
International safety restraint systems manufacturer with annual sales of $750MM and over 27 worldwide locations.

Sr. Vice President, Human Resources - Member of Executive Management Team, Executive Strategic Planning Committee, Executive Acquisition Team and Corporate liaison to the Board of Director's Compensation Committee.
   ◇ Key member of Cardiff's Initial Public Offering team.
   ◇ Senior Compliance Officer (Business Code of Conduct).
   ◇ Trustee, Japanese, U.K. Pension Schemes and U.S. 40l(k) programs.

Designed and established a Corporate Human Resource function with a worldwide performance appraisal, salary administration, and short/long term incentive program and the company's first Safety, Health and Environmental department.

- Recruited an executive team to penetrate the automotive market and established two manufacturing facilities in eighteen months.

- Designed and established corporate-wide health and welfare programs, consolidating existing program while upgrading flexibility/quality and reducing costs.

- Created and directed a recruitment effort which managed the company's growth from 42 to over 8,750 employees in eight years.

- Supervised the implementation of two Human Resource Information Systems that boosted productivity and provided ease of access and report-generation by all HR staff.

- Established domestic and offshore labor relations programs that maintained a union-free environment and strike-free operations in the collective bargaining units.

- Designed corporate-wide management development program, succession plan, skill-based training programs and supervisory training program; all directly impacted the ability to obtain BSI's QS-9000 certification and single digit part per million ratings.

MEGA GLOBE CORPORATION, Braintree, MA   1984 - 1988
International telecommunications manufacturer of protection and connection devices to the new Bell Operating Companies, with operations in Korea, England, Mexico, Czechoslovakia, Puerto Rico, Chile and Argentina.

Vice President of Administration/Director of Administration
Created the corporate human resource operation in the United States, Puerto Rico, England and Mexico.

- Established corporate-wide salary administration program, performance appraisal program, H.R.I.S., management development program and management incentive plan.
  - Designed, implemented and managed all health and welfare programs.
  - Maintained non-union status in the U.S. while structuring operations in Mexico.
  - Established first policy and procedures manual and business code of ethics.
  - Created Safety and Security programs to ensure compliance for all facets of business in the United States, Puerto Rico, England and Mexico.

MARS CHEMICAL CORPORATION, Wilmington, DE   1981 - 1984
Specialty chemicals manufacturer with operations, sales and distribution centers located throughout the United States, Europe and the Far East.

Manager, Management Development
Established first management development function and implemented the first international performance appraisal/salary administration program. Directed all technical and management training activities.
  - Managed corporate-wide "MBO" program.
  - Chaired cross-functional project team to open a new plant in Indonesia.

ST. CHRISTOPHER's SCHOOL, Dobbs Ferry, NY   1970 - 1981
Agency serving dependent/neglected, emotionally disturbed children in residential treatment centers.

Unit Supervisor/Unit Director/Associate Director
Recruited, interviewed and hired professional and non-professional staff. Created the first management development program. Directed/managed budgeting and contract administration.

JEWISH CHILD CARE ASS'N., Brooklyn, NY   1968 - 1970
Residential program for emotionally disturbed children in metropolitan New York.

Group Home Supervisor/Child Care Worker

EDUCATION/PROFESSIONAL AFFILIATIONS

Human Resource Executive Program, Harvard University, Boston, MA   1995
M.A., Education, Marist College, Poughkeepsie, NY   1971
B.A., Marymount College, Tarrytown, NY   1968

Society For Human Resource Management
American Compensation Association
University of Tennessee School of Continuing Education, Adjunct Professor
Hamilton County Executive Human Resource Round Table

Power Resume Tip

Keep line length as short as possible. Studies have proven that it is easier to read information that's laid out in a longer block of copy with shorter lines than a short block of copy with long lines.

The One-Stop Shopping Place

Bring Immediate Attention to Your Skills

John Suarez, director of career services for The Resume Center, a St. Louis-area career marketing company, selected this resume from the many he's worked with because of its successful combination of graphic design and information.

"Lance has a strong systems administration background as well as a broad knowledge of general software applications," explains Suarez. "The headline-style objective, with buzzword tag lines sprinkled underneath, draws the reader in to the summary paragraph that follows, which goes into more detail."

In addition, a partially shaded box brings immediate attention to Lance's technical skills, giving the prospective employer a one-stop shopping place to visually scan Lance's background by category.

"His most recent computer-related position is not current, yet it is listed first to bring out those skills," adds Suarez. "Lance's current position is listed afterward as 'Additional Experience.'"

The career consultant chose to highlight Lance's accomplishments in a separate section to demonstrate skills that would appear to be above and beyond the actual job title. The incomplete degree program is mentioned simply as course work in the Education section.

John A. Suarez, CPRW
Director of Career Services, The Resume Center

As director of career services, John Suarez manages all retail services, marketing, relocation assistance, outplacement, community service, outside consulting and public relations for The Resume Center.

Suarez also is staff consultant for Exec-U-Net, a national career management and networking organization for senior-level executives, an adjunct college instructor for professional development and communication courses and a corporate trainer for business writing courses at Ralston Purina Company.

He is an award-winning communicator who has been recognized for his expertise in creative resume writing and design by the Professional Association of Resume Writers. Suarez is a nationally published and Certified Professional Resume Writer (CPRW). He can be reached at his e-mail address: JASuarez@aol.com

Lance Hillary

140 Damian Court • Belleville, Illinois 62220 • (618) 555-3332

Office Automation / Systems Administrator

LAN and PC Support...Software Testing & Evaluation
Technical Training...Data Security

Versatile technical background as the sole system administrator and key resource for a 15-member office supporting primarily environmental research functions. Proven ability to plan, evaluate, troubleshoot, test, and install automated systems used to increase office efficiency and simplify end-user applications. Experienced at writing technical instructions and customizing database and report formats.

Operated and/or evaluated the following:

Software	Enable, Word, WordStar, MultiMate Advantage II, PeachText
Spreadsheets	Excel, Quattro Pro, Lotus Express
Hardware	Compaq PC, Zenith Z-100/Z-248/486-DX, CD-ROM, Cabling, Workstations, File Servers, Network Interface Cards, HP Printers
Graphics	Harvard Graphics, PowerPoint, Paintbrush
Databases	dBASE IV/V, FoxPro, Access
Communications	DaVinci E-mail, ProComm Plus, WinfaxPro
Operating Systems	MS-DOS, Windows (including Windows '95), Novell

Professional Experience

BIOENVIRONMENTAL ENGINEERING SERVICES, Scott Air Force Base, Illinois   1989-1994
Office Automation Assistant

Identify information processes suitable for automating using packaged software or designing and developing new databases and report formats. Train and oversee a 15-member staff using a variety of software packages. Document data entry and retrieval procedures.

Install new software and configure as required by system characteristics. Setup menus, write short batch routines, and resolve problems related to text formatting, data manipulation, structured retrievals, and disk directories.

Monitor work in progress to detect unusual computer delays and unforeseen problems. Monitor and adjust routine priorities: queuing printers, clearing in-use conditions, and disconnecting peripherals to free them for other applications.

Key Accomplishments:

- Researched and wrote a local area network (LAN) acquisition package for Aeromedical Services. Identified and ordered all necessary cables, components, and hubs. Evaluated software, hardware, and systems requirements. Tested, setup, and coordinated operation with other LAN's.

- Installed CD-ROM; downloaded data and configured proprietary information management system to interface with CD-ROM data. Track data pertaining to safety/occupational hazards and hazardous materials. Configured printers to respond to program changes.

- Served as the Terminal Area Security Officer. Attended meetings to maintain currency on required policies. Distributed information regarding data security and integrity.

Additional Experience (1994-Present): Currently working as a marketing director for an insurance company; ranked in top 5% of company.

Education

BELLEVILLE AREA COLLEGE, Belleville, Illinois
Associate of Arts Degree Coursework in Computer Science

References Available Upon Request

The New Federal Resume

So Long to the Cumbersome SF-171

The federal government has eliminated the long, cumbersome SF-171 and now gives applicants the choice of using a "federal" resume.

"There are several major differences (noted in the shaded areas) between a federal resume and a private industry resume," explains Kathryn Troutman, president of The Resume Place in Washington, D.C., and Baltimore, Md. "These 'compliance' details are required for security reasons and are listed in the Office of Personnel Management's flyer, the OF-510. If you don't include these details, you will lose consideration for the position."

Roberta Spencer's resume comes from Troutman's federal resume books, *Reinvention Federal Resumes* and *The Federal Resume Guidebook* (published by The Resume Place).

Troutman also includes the first page of Spencer's resume as it looks when prepared as a federal e-mail text resume.

"This is the format you must follow for the new Resumix scanning recruitment processes some government agencies are using," says the expert. "Other agencies will soon follow. Your text resume can be a maximum of three pages. Agencies require that your e-mail resume be in text format and include the federal compliance details."

Kathryn Troutman
President, The Resume Place

Kathryn Troutman founded The Resume Place in 1971 to provide professional resume and federal application writing services for the nation's capital and U.S.-wide government and private industry clients. Her most recent book, *The Federal Resume Guidebook,* details how to write an effective federal resume and covers the new federal employment process.

For more information on federal resumes, federal job openings, Resumix and scanning, see her Web site at http://www.resumeplace.com/jobs

---

ROBERTA E. SPENCER
124 3rd Street, NE,
Washington, DC 20002

Home: (202) 567-8910   Work: (202) 267-9976

Social Security Number: 345-87-6540   *Veteran's Status:* N/A
Federal Civilian Status: Public Affairs Specialist, GS-12   *Citizenship:* U.S.

OBJECTIVE: International Aviation Operations Specialist, AWA-AIA-96-1379-10590

PROFILE: Aviation communications professional with over 15 years experience demonstrating organizational skills, award-winning media relations, and development and maintenance of positive relationships among government employees, industry representatives, and academia. Recent assignments include special project involving Pacific region air transportation technology and multiple agency missions. Adept at reviewing, analyzing, and maintaining government and private industry programs, budgets, and collateral materials with international effects.

RECENT ACCOMPLISHMENTS

- Facilitated international meetings of Chinese, Filipino, Indian, and Pakistani media briefings after negotiations of air traffic control protocols for Pacific Ocean flights. Prepared briefing materials and agendas, organized presentations, and ensured complete media access to technical officials. Presentations resulted in major international coverage for innovative technologies in air commerce.

- Completed developmental assignment with U.S. Customs Service to publicize strengthened enforcement of smuggling laws with regard to major Asian nations. Coordinated presentations for international meetings involving Maylasian, Pakistani, and Filipino governments and presenting resolution of complex international negotiations.

- Published articles in *FAA World* describing agency perspective on success of international negotiations. Reported advances in air traffic control technology, new agreement with the Peoples' Republic of China for maintenance of aircraft consistent with FAA standards, and new international smuggling accord.

PROFESSIONAL EXPERIENCE:

FEDERAL AVIATION ADMINISTRATION   October 1991 to Present
800 Independence Avenue, SW   40 hrs./week
Washington, DC 20591   Starting Salary: $35,136
Supervisor: Roger Sperrin (202) 267-9975   Current Salary: $47,154
You may contact present employer

Deputy Public Affairs Officer, GS-12/4   October 1993 to Present

Represent FAA Headquarters before general media in the absence of the Public Affairs Officer. Coordinated seven-person branch providing public information about the agency's mission, policies, and operations to ensure timely and responsive presentation of sensitive issues of aviation policy and technology. Earned recognition from print and electronic media for professionalism of briefings and quick responses to technical topics.

Managed month-long detail in FAA's Los Angeles Public Affairs Office to provide major market coverage of sensitive issues involving U.S. agencies and Asian-Pacific nations. Achieved substantial public awareness of impact of new trade agreements on international transportation systems.

Public Affairs Specialist, GS-1035-11/12   October 1991 - 1993
FAA Aviation Education Program Manager   40 hrs./week
Supervisor: William Leytle (202) 267-8338   Starting Salary: $29,876
                                                                   Ending Salary: $31,352

Edited weekly employee newsletter electronically disseminated to 2,735 Washington-area FAA employees. Established systematic procedures to solicit reader input and produce a cost-effective product that kept employees knowledgeable about agency issues and programs. Innovations in on-line production technology cut distribution time by one-third while realizing 20 percent cost savings.

Promoted and encouraged partnerships with businesses, education, and government organizations involving aviation activities. Enhanced development of a multi-agency commitment to the aviation education program that reached several thousand students each year. New pilot licensing in Headquarters region increased 7 percent annually during this program.

Developed and implemented budgetary requirements and procedures for media campaigns. Scheduled annual calendar for the Public Affairs Office. Devised and implemented components and timelines for strengthened general aviation safety concepts in FAA's Aviation Education program. Campaign cited by AOPA for reducing general aviation accident rate during 1993.

Conducted investigative interviews with employees and members of the media to provide technical background related to revised air traffic control procedures resulting from new airport radar systems at metropolitan Washington airports.

DEPARTMENT OF DEFENSE   October 1988 - 1991
Pacific Air Command   40 hrs./week
The Pentagon, Washington, DC 20330   Starting Salary: $24,865
Supervisor: Rod Serling (202) 737-8637   Ending Salary: $27,546

Assistant Command Historian, GS-9

Coordinated three-member team conducting interviews with military leaders at Air Force Bases for annual historical records maintained under classified conditions. These histories averaged 800 pages in length with an equal number of pages of supporting documents. Secured and monitored publication contracts for multi-volume editions.

Organized 50th anniversary reunion of more than 100 veterans from the 11th Air Force who fought in Hawaii during World War II. The event included three days of activities on Pearl Harbor Naval Station and highlighted a 45-minute video featuring many of the attendees in vintage film footage. Arranged lodging, meals, and transportation, and conducted exit interviews with 80 percent of participants before departure. Convention cited by Air Force Association Historical Society.

Research Historian   September, 1985 - 1988
Hawaii Naval Air Station, Honolulu, HI   40 hrs./week
Supervisor: Mr. John Clayton (808) 546-7785   Starting Salary: $21,156
                                                                   Ending Salary: $23,652

Reviewed development and implementation of air transportation systems supporting Allied Pacific operations during World War II. Historical research developed full documentation of aircraft, airport, and airway support technologies used to integrate multinational air, sea, and land forces.

EDUCATION & TRAINING:

Bachelor of Arts (Speech & Communications)	**University of California-Los Angeles** Los Angeles, CA 95701	June 1971
Diploma	**Robert Fulton High School** Queens, NY 10065	June 1967

PROFESSIONAL DEVELOPMENT/TRAINING:

> ### *U.S.D.A. Graduate School*   1995-1996
> *Aviation Executive Leadership Program*
> Mentor: Charlene Derry (907) 271-5534
> Successfully completed developmental assignments emphasizing leadership and management potential. Formalized classroom training included leadership styles, managing conflict, empowerment, stress, and cultural diversity management. Cluster group assignments focused on improving performance management in a team environment.
>
> - Assistant to FAA's International Liaison Officer for 60 days in planning and performance of multi-national meetings developing protocols to shift air traffic control technology over Pacific Ocean routes. Coordinated media presence in three-day international meetings, securing substantial favorable coverage for the U.S. government and the agency.
>
> - Assisted the Resident Agent-in-Charge with the U.S. Customs Office for 30 days. Managed public affairs for international smuggling conference, providing important coverage for new international law enforcement protocols governing movement of passengers and freight. Supported operation through media expertise and technical familiarity with airspace system operations.
>
> ### *Other Professional Courses*
> **Aviation Technical Courses:**
> Detail, FAA Civil Aviation Security Office (1995)
> Introduction to Emergency Readiness (1995)
> Air Traffic Control History (1994)
> Managing Public Communication, FAA Center for Management Development (1993)
>
> **Management Development Courses:** (All 1994)
> Seven Habits of Highly Effective People   The Quality Advantage
> Management Skills for Non-Supervisors   Investment in Excellence
> Discovering Diversity/Valuing the Diverse Workforce   Thinking Beyond the Boundaries
>
> **Communications Training:**
> Public Involvement Training (1991)
> Collateral Duty Recruiter Training (1990)
> Constructive Communications (1988)
> Communications Training Workshop (1989)

RECENT PROFESSIONAL PUBLICATIONS:

> Co-author, ***Woman & Minorities in Aviation in Hawaii,*** Hawaii Office of Education, 1994
> "Aviation Progress in the Pacific," ***FAA World***, October 1995
> "Safety Basics for the Novice Pilot," ***Aviation Education News***, Fall 1993
> ***Our Hawaii***, marketing book used worldwide by private corporation in Hawaii, 1988
> ***The Air War in the Pacific***, (Honolulu, Air Force Historical Association), 1987

PROFESSIONAL MEMBERSHIPS & AFFILIATIONS:

> Air Traffic Advisory Committee
> Air Force Association
> Hawaii Aerospace Development Corporation
> Federal Women's Program
> Civil Air Patrol Aviation Education and Professional Development Committee
> Honolulu Chamber of Commerce

HONORS & AWARDS:

> Outstanding Performance Ratings seven consecutive years   1989 - 1995
> National Award for Excellence in Aerospace Education from Civil Air Patrol (Brewer Award)   1995

Sample Scannable Federal Resume - Text Format for E-Mail.

ROBERTA E. SPENCER
124 3rd Street, NE
Washington, DC 20002
Home: (202) 567-8910
Work: (202) 267-9976
Social Security Number: 345-87-6540
Veteran's Status: N/A
Federal Civilian Status: Public Affairs Specialist, GS-12
Citizenship: U.S.

OBJECTIVE: International Aviation Operations Specialist, AWA-AIA-96-1379-10590

PROFILE: Aviation communications professional with over 15 years experience
demonstrating organizational skills, award-winning media relations, and
development and maintenance of positive relationships among government
employees, industry representatives, and academia. Recent assignments include
special project involving Pacific region air transportation technology and
multiple agency missions. Adept at reviewing, analyzing, and maintaining
government and private industry programs, budgets, and collateral materials with
international effects.

RECENT ACCOMPLISHMENTS:
Facilitated international meetings of Chinese, Filipino, Indian, and Pakistani
media briefings after negotiations of air traffic control protocols for Pacific
Ocean flights. Prepared briefing materials and agendas, organized
presentations, and ensured complete media access to technical officials.
Presentations resulted in major international coverage for innovative
technologies in air commerce.

Completed developmental assignment with U.S. Customs Service to publicize
strengthened enforcement of smuggling laws with regard to major Asian nations.
Coordinated presentations for international meetings involving Malaysian,
Pakistani, and Filipino governments and presenting resolution of complex
international negotiations.

Published articles in FAA World describing agency perspective on success of
international negotiations. Reported advances in air traffic control technology,
new agreement with the Peoples' Republic of China for maintenance of aircraft
consistent with FAA standards, and new international smuggling accord.

PROFESSIONAL EXPERIENCE:

FEDERAL AVIATION ADMINISTRATION
800 Independence Avenue, SW, Washington, DC 20591
October 1991 to Present

Deputy Public Affairs Officer, GS-12/4
October 1993 to Present
40 hrs./week
Starting Salary: $35,136
Current Salary: $47,154
Supervisor: Roger Sperrin (202) 267-9975
You may contact present employer

Represent FAA Headquarters before general media in the absence of the Public
Affairs Officer. Coordinated seven-person branch providing public information
about the agency's mission, policies, and operations to ensure timely and
responsive presentation of sensitive issues of aviation policy and technology.

Power Resume Tip

Make sure you are consistent throughout your resume. Be sure to use the same line spacing, headline treatment, listing treatment, etc.

The Creation of a Successful Marketing Tool

Ten Steps to a Winning Resume

"When you are developing a resume, the primary goal is the creation of a successful marketing tool which showcases the client's selling points to the potential 'buyer,'" says Vicki Bacal, president of The Resume Specialist in Minneapolis.

Kelly Mason's resume, with its innovative Career Highlights format and eye-catching Expertise section, illustrates Bacal's basic rules quite well. Many of Bacal's clients have generated a great response using this format. The resume should:

1. Address the reader's needs, answering the question, "Why should I hire you?" Note Mason's "Resourceful manager, skilled in staff training and motivation."

2. Highlight outstanding characteristics in a rapid-fire Summary of Qualifications to provide a quick overview. Note use of "Accomplished Business Professional" and "proven record of timely completion."

3. Tell the reader how you made a difference. Note Mason's "achieved optimal settlements at minimal cost to company" and "Educated managers of 1200 stores."

4. Be clear, concise and specific. Use facts and figures to add credibility.

5. Emphasize your key accomplishments with short sentences and descriptive action verbs to gain and hold reader attention. Note Mason's use of "initiated and developed the first Customer Service Department."

6. Use repetition of key ideas to remind the reader of your greatest strengths and achievements. Note repetition of "effective communication," "cost efficiency" and "problem solving."

7. Let the reader know that you understand the industry by using insider terminology. Note use of "streamlining expenses," "detailed investigation" and "claims management."

8. Use attractive graphics, white space, underlining and boldface to draw reader interest.

9. Highlight on-the-job and continuing education to emphasize current knowledge and augment undergraduate education.

10. Take credit for your role in successful projects. Note Mason's many examples of leadership, initiative and accomplishment.

Vicki Bacal, M.A.
The Resume Specialist

Vicki Bacal has advised more than 10,000 clients nationwide since 1985 in the areas of resume writing, interview preparation and job-search strategy. With a background in public relations and higher education, she brings a marketing-oriented approach to client projects. Bacal is a keynote speaker at the annual *Star Tribune* Career Expo, a frequent seminar leader and a consultant to the Women's Employment Resource Center.

15007 Spring Lake Road Edina, MN 55439	**KELLY A. MASON**	Residence: 612-900-4286 Office: 612-300-8231

SUMMARY of PROFESSIONAL QUALIFICATIONS

- **Accomplished Business Professional** with demonstrated history of quality performance and leadership in a fast paced environment.
- Highly effective in negotiation, problem solving and analysis.
- Experienced in all aspects of claims management; proven record of timely completion and customer satisfaction.
- Resourceful manager skilled in staff training and motivation.
- Dedicated and dependable; committed to cost efficiency.

EXPERTISE

- **Settlement Negotiations**
- **Customer Relations**
- **Creative Problem Solving**
- **Claims Investigation**
- **Personnel Management**
- **Interpersonal Communication**

CAREER HIGHLIGHTS

Negotiated and settled major property and casualty claims through detailed investigation, careful analysis and effective communication; consistently achieved optimal settlements at minimal cost to company.

Interacted effectively with insurance companies, attorneys, and claimants nationwide to quickly obtain information and resolve issues.

Successfullly initiated and developed the first Customer Service Department at Premier Corporation; hired and trained a highly effective service team which significantly improved response to customer needs.

Analyzed monthly/annual profit and loss statements, sales and payroll reports for over 200 stores, recommending immediate action.

Commended by management for streamlining expenses through effective budget control, store oversight and expense monitoring.

EXPERIENCE

PREMIER CORPORATION, Minneapolis, MN
Industry leader with $500 million in annual revenues.
Operations Coordinator 1993 to Present
- Provide strong operational support to Regional Managers, Area Supervisors and other managers; received annual monetary bonuses.
- Conduct annual Manager's Meetings, traveling throughout Southeast Region. Deliver presentations on cost control and expense management.

Claims Representative/Customer Service Manager 1986 to 1993
- Investigated, evaluated and negotiated casualty/property claims.
- Created and implemented all Claims Department policies/procedures.
- Worked with insurance carriers and attorneys to resolve claims.
- Directed and motivated Customer Service team.
- Educated managers of 1200 stores in efficient handling of customer complaints; designed and distributed quality informational materials.

Payroll Coordinator 1985 to 1986

EDUCATION

UNIVERSITY OF MINNESOTA, Minneapolis, MN
Coursework in:
- *Insurance*
- *Risk Management*
- *Legal Issues*
- *Personnel Supervision*
- *Effective Communication*
- *Customer Service*

NORTH HENNEPIN COMMUNITY COLLEGE, Brooklyn Park, MN
Associate of Arts Degree, in progress

COMPUTER

IBM PC
- *Windows*
- *Microsoft Office*
- *WordPerfect*
- *dBase*
- *Lotus 1-2-3*
- *Quicken*

Functional *and* Effective

You Can Have It Both Ways

"A functional resume *can* be effective," says Beth Stefani, owner of Resumes, Etc., in Hamburg, N.Y.

"This resume helped Roberta Carson secure an interview with a manufacturer and distributor of specialized medical equipment," she adds. "She's currently working there as the director of human resources."

Up until her most recent position, Roberta's career in human resources had been narrowly focused in the area of benefits administration. At Riverside Technologies, Inc., she expanded her skills and experience in employee relations and compensation/salary administration.

"To highlight her abilities in all three areas, we chose a combined functional/chronological resume format," Stefani says.

The first page draws attention to Roberta's greatest strengths and interests. The horizontal lines and the crisp looking "small cap" font style used on category headings draw attention to each section, adding a bold, eye-catching appearance to the resume. Her employment history and other pertinent information can be found on the second page. And with the clean, direct and appealing look of the resume, readers are sure to turn to the second page—and keep reading.

Beth W. Stefani, Ed.M., MBA
Owner/Consultant, Resumes, Etc.

Resumes, Etc., located in Hamburg, N.Y., specializes in custom-designed resumes and cover letters, career counseling and job search advisement. In addition to providing individual assistance to job hunters on a personal referral basis, Stefani is a consultant with RW Caldwell Associates, Inc., a corporate-sponsored outplacement and career management firm in Buffalo, N.Y. Previously, she worked in commercial lending and credit analysis at Marine Midland Bank and Chase Manhattan Bank in Buffalo, N.Y. Earlier, as a career counselor at the State University of New York at Buffalo, Stefani managed the campus recruitment program for business and engineering graduates.

ROBERTA D. CARSON

1234 Elm Street • *Clarence Center, New York 14032* • *Residence: (716) 555-5555*

SUMMARY OF QUALIFICATIONS

Human resources professional skilled in benefits administration, including thrift / 401(k) plans, ESOP, defined benefit and defined compensation plans, and pension calculations. Also qualified to manage salary administration, compensation, and employee relations / communications. Excellent people skills with a highly confidential nature. Proficient in computer word processing, spreadsheet, and database programs.

BENEFITS ADMINISTRATION

- Managed benefits administration for headquarters and up to eight off-site locations, requiring extensive travel and telephone communications with all levels of employees.
- Experienced in researching and purchasing outside insured medical, dental, life insurance, AD & D, disability, and flexible spending benefit programs.
- Authored company policies and administered the benefit programs after completion.
- Implemented the Human Resources Information System (H.R.I.S.) developed by Hewitt Associates.
- Experienced in working with Thrift/401(k) Plans for union and non-union employees.
- Aided management in conversion of salaried benefit structure of medical plan from outside insurance company to self-insured benefit. Monitored state and federal compliance.
- Conducted group and individual new hire orientations; led discussion groups addressing personnel issues and benefits.
- Served on Independent Health Employer Advisory Council.

EMPLOYEE RELATIONS

- Served as liaison to improve and expand communications between management and union personnel.
- Addressed and resolved employee problems and concerns regarding their individual benefits packages.
- Authored monthly "Benefits News" newsletter for employees and retirees. Wrote articles on long-term disability benefits, 401(k) savings plan alternatives, flexible spending accounts, medical and dental plan alternatives, pension planning, and short-term disability.
- Established a committee to identify basic employee benefits concerns and issues.
- Initiated "Benefits Express" telecommunications hotline for benefits information. Coordinated updating of employee database with Hewitt Associates, Inc.
- Wrote articles, compiled, and edited company magazine distributed to all divisions.
- Created and led periodic "brown bag" lunch hour discussions and subsequent day-long seminars regarding pre-retirement planning, financial planning, wellness, social security benefits, and long term health care insurance, utilizing outside and internal experts when needed.
- Organized annual "Take our Daughters to Work" day in conjunction with nationally recognized event. Recognized as one of the first area companies to take part in the event.

Compensation / Salary Administration

- Established salary grades and levels for new hires, promotions, within guidelines.
- Created job descriptions, educational and experience requirements, and salary grades/ranges for newly created positions.
- Coordinated annual merit procedures and matched departmental performance reviews with merit budget. Conducted human resources survey to obtain national, local, and internal merit guidelines.
- Wrote proposal for "broad band" compensation program to be utilized company-wide.

Employment History

RIVERSIDE TECHNOLOGIES INC., Buffalo, New York   1989 - 1997
High technology organization providing research/development and testing/evaluation services to government, military, and commercial customers.

Human Resources Benefits Representative

SENLIN CORP., Williamsville, New York   1982 - 1989
Manufacturer of chemicals and other products for the automobile and consumer products industries.

Benefits Administrator

BESSIMER CHEMICAL SUPPLY, Lockport, New York   1980 - 1982
Diversified manufacturer supplying raw materials, chemical products, technology, and engineering services.

Benefits Administrator - Headquarters Office, Lockport, New York (1980 - 1982)
Benefits Clerk - Employment Office - Licol Division, Tonawanda, New York (1974 - 1980)

Computer Skills

Proficient in Windows applications of Microsoft Works, Microsoft Word, and Excel, QuatroPro. Extensive use of Human Resources Information Systems (H.R.I.S.).

Education

B.S., BUSINESS ADMINISTRATION, State University of New York at Buffalo, 1991

A.A.S., BUSINESS ADMINISTRATION, Bryant & Stratton Business Institute, 1985

Attended professional seminars on the following human resources topics: Compensation, labor relations, age and discrimination laws, and employee publications/newsletters.

Power Resume Tip

Proofread your resume several times. Remember, if the resume you submit to your prospective employer isn't completely error-free, you might as well kiss the job good-bye.

Take Flight from the Pigeonhole

A Resume That Acts as a Change Agent

"This candidate's objective was to change careers," notes Lauri Ann Plante, senior career management consultant for Right Associates in Philadelphia. "Therefore, a functional resume was his best option for highlighting accomplishments he gained from work and nonwork experiences.

"A chronological resume," continues Plante, "would have pigeonholed this person in a field he no longer wished to be in and would not have clearly identified his other strengths."

Steven J. Company achieved his money-management know-how strictly by handling his own finances and working with friends and family. His work experience had no relation to what he now saw as his career goal, which is stated clearly in his Objective paragraph.

"Notice how his professional affiliation helps validate his credentials as a highly motivated, well-organized business leader," points out Plante. "His accomplishments are enough to whet the appetite of any prospective employer."

Lauri Ann Plante, SPHR
Senior Career Management Consultant, Right Associates

At Right Associates, Lauri Plante is responsible for managing the professionals on the firm's project staff team. A human resources professional with more than 15 years' experience, primarily in financial services, Plante's career emphasis has been in recruitment and employee relations at both field and corporate levels. In addition to her work with individual candidates at Right Associates, she has conducted workshops for numerous corporations to assist their employees in career transition.

Plante is a Senior Professional in Human Resources (SPHR), a designation awarded by the Human Resources Certification Institute, the credentialing body founded by the Society for Human Resources Management (SHRM). She serves as delegate to the New Jersey State Council of SHRM and chairs Membership At Large for southern New Jersey.

Prior to joining Right Associates, Plante implemented the first field human resource function at City Federal Savings and Loan and pioneered recruitment efforts in a ground-floor operation at The Traveler's Mortgage Services corporate offices.

She has been featured in *Who's Who of American Women* and was nominated into *Who's Who of Emerging Leaders*. She is a frequent guest speaker on various career management issues.

STEVEN J. COMPANY

123 XYZ Lane
Medford, NJ 08123
(609) 555-5555

OBJECTIVE

A position in which financial planning skills can be used to help clients increase wealth over the long term through the use of appropriate investment strategies and vehicles.

BACKGROUND

A highly motivated, self-taught personal investment strategist, with ten years of successful results in developing individual financial plans. Well-organized business manager. Well versed and experienced in a broad spectrum of issues in personal money management, including:

- Retirement
- Insurance
- Stocks and bonds
- Short and long range strategies
- Family budgeting
- Savings
- Mutual Funds

PROFESSIONAL ACCOMPLISHMENTS

- Improved personal finances from state of debt to one of substantial net worth, through methodical research, observation, and application of sound investment principles.
- Developed and refined a system of reliable, proven rules for personal investing which avoid common investment mistakes.
- Designed successful investment strategies for individual clients in a wide variety of age brackets and income groups with sensitivity to a diversity of individual goals, priorities and attitudes towards risk.
- Conducted seminars in various aspects of financial planning and investing, as organizer and leader of investment club.
- Consistent reader and student of numerous financial publications.
- Gained reputation for sound, conservative investment counsel, with high success rate of client follow through on advice given.

EMPLOYMENT

THE RETAIL CHAIN, Merion, NJ   1991 - 1997

Distribution Center Supervisor

GQC CORPORATION , Princeton, NJ   1980 - 1991

Supervisor

BLUE, GREEN & YELLOW PUBLISHING, Austin, TX   1980

Crew Chief

EDUCATION

B.A., Political Science
University of Florida, Gainesville, FL

AFFILIATIONS

- Vice Chairman Board of Directors, Junior Achievement
- Chairman of Selective Service Board of Hope County
- Board of Trustees, Congregation of Good People, Medford Lakes, NJ

After the Cap and Gown

A Resume for the Recent Graduate

"This resume is a good example for a recent college graduate," says Marlyn Kalitan, vice president, career management for Right Management Consultants. "Your goal as a recent graduate is to build up the reader's expectations of your qualifications based on the skills you've demonstrated in your part-time jobs. Kim's resume is especially fun to read because, if you look closely, you'll see she has no real paid work experience."

However, Kim constructs a resume that clearly highlights skills she developed during her student teaching and summer jobs, all valuable experiences. Her background summary gives a good indication of her qualifications. Kim makes good use of action verbs and, when possible, notes positive results of her actions. She is currently enrolled in a master's degree program and therefore is looking only for a part-time position, which she states in her objective.

Kalitan offers these other tips to those getting ready to enter the job market:

- Use action-oriented verbs and stay away from phrases such as "responsible for." Tell the reader *what* you did and the *results* of those actions.

- If your GPA is less than 3.0, don't list it. Kim uses hers because it's a fairly good one.

Marlyn Kalitan
Vice President, Career Management
Right Management Consultants

Marlyn Kalitan, vice president, career management, has been with Right Management Consultants, a world-wide consulting firm, since 1983. She has extensive experience in business, teaching and career counseling, and has provided numerous re-employment, consulting and entrepreneurship workshops.

Kalitan provides one-on-one job search coaching and career transition assistance to individuals at all management levels in a variety of industries. She also works with individuals in change management and leadership effectiveness and with organizations to plan strategic directions and provide executive coaching.

In 1995, she received the Chairman's Award in recognition of being voted the number-one consultant in the company. Prior to joining Right Management, Kalitan was sole proprietor of a consulting firm and involved in a family-owned business. A frequent guest speaker at professional organizations and conferences, she is former vice president of professional development for the Philadelphia Chapter of the National Human Resources Association.

136 Main Street
Apple Hill, NJ 00000
(609) 555-555

OBJECTIVE   A part-time position utilizing strong organizational, interpersonal and communication skills.

SUMMARY OF   Extensive experience in supervising children, including:
QUALIFICATIONS

- Developing and organizing activities
- Creating arts and crafts projects
- Improving skills
- Motivating students

EXPERIENCE

ABC SCHOOL, Pennsauken, NJ   1997
Student Teacher
Formulated lesson plans, created bulletin boards, taught third grade in a self-contained classroom, and improved classroom management.

- Designed Learning Centers to increase students' awareness of the learning process.

DEFG SCHOOL, Mt. Laurel, NJ   1996
Student Practicum
Performed all duties associated with teaching fifth grade in a self-contained classroom and observed teacher-student interaction.

SUN DAY CAMP, Medford, NJ   **Summers, 1991-1996**
Senior Counselor   1994-1996
Supervised approximately 18 eight to nine year old campers. Planned and organized activities, conducted conferences with parents, initiated innovative programming and strengthened coordination skills.

- Selected as "Color War" Captain to plan and implement a 22-team athletic competition.

Junior Counselor   1991-1993
Assisted senior counselor in coordinating all camp activities.

- Motivated children to participate in all individual and team-based programs.

EDUCATION

B.A., Elementary Education, Rowan University, Glassboro, NJ   1997
G.P.A. 3.2/4.0
Currently enrolled in Master's Degree Program at **Rowan University**.

A Record That Speaks for Itself

A Resume Approach That's Definitely Not for Everyone

"This resume is the most unusual, yet effective, that ever crossed my desk," says Robert Half, founder of Robert Half International Inc., one of the world's largest personnel recruiting firms. "It has only 36 words. However, it landed the candidate eight interviews from which he got four job offers in a short period of time."

You can hardly argue with such success!

"Since the candidate was applying for a position as an accountant," notes Half, "those companies that viewed the resume were fully familiar with the quality of his experience and education. In addition, the resume clearly points out his achievement—the most important feature of any resume."

This candidate graduated from top schools with high grades and earned a senior accountant position within three years. This, indeed, is a record that, as Half says, "speaks for itself."

Half also points out that this resume contains "no reference to goals, but in my opinion such statements are generally not necessary on a resume and often tend to eliminate qualified candidates who include goals that might be too limited."

The advantages of this very short and sweet approach? "Well," says Half, "it will be read in its entirety by almost everyone. It contains all the essential facts. It establishes the candidate's successes. And it's professional, yet novel."

Robert Half
Founder, Robert Half International Inc.

Although he founded one of the most renowned personnel recruiting firms more than 40 years ago, Robert Half is still an active voice in the area of careers and job search. His latest book is *Finding, Hiring, and Keeping The Best Employees*, now in paperback from John Wiley & Sons, Inc. Robert Half International Inc. specializes in accounting and financial professionals through Accountemps, its temporary placement service, and its Robert Half division. The company has more than 175 offices and is listed on the New York Stock Exchange.

Charles Ridley, CPA

123 Monadnock Road
Newton, MA 02167

| Harvard | BA | 1991 * |
| Harvard | MBA | 1993 * |

* Graduated top 15%

1993 to 1996—Brown, Gray & Co., Big Six CPA firm.
Achieved Senior Accountant status in three years.

Accentuate the Positive

A Resume for a Declining Job Market

Susan's resume was written to help her continue as a programmer in a main-frame environment, a shrinking field with the advent of powerful PCs, says the staff of Russell-Rogat Transition Specialists, Inc.

Her work experience has been with one company, and Susan's resume shows her solid career growth over those 20 years. The staff points out that she has the added advantage of showing the personal growth resulting from recent returns to school for both undergraduate and graduate degrees.

Because Susan's career objective is very clear, an objective statement would be appropriate. However, the staff elected to exclude it so that the reader can immediately focus on the special set of competencies Susan brings to a programmer position.

Staff of
Russell-Rogat Transition Specialists, Inc.

Founded in 1984, Russell-Rogat Transition Specialists, Inc., in Cleveland, Ohio, provides corporate-sponsored services in outplacement, career development, work force transition, spouse relocation assistance and pre-retirement planning programs. Through its work, the firm provides customized programs to assist employees in managing career change and the resulting transition process. Its motto, "From Beginning to Beginning," represents the view that the beginning of a change can lead to the beginning of a new opportunity. Russell-Rogat is a member of the Association of Outplacement Consulting Firms International.

SUSAN B. LEWIS

| 1223 Gilford Avenue | Bay Village, Ohio 44140 | (216) 555-7111 |

CAREER SUMMARY:

Master's prepared programmer with 12 years of experience and strengths in troubleshooting and interpersonal skills. Extensive background in applying technical skills across organizational boundaries. Attitude and demeanor that contribute to successful results. Computer skills include:

➢SAR	➢Windows 95	➢IBM Compatible PC
➢JCL	➢CICS	➢Line Printer Operations
➢COBOL	➢Microsoft Excel	➢TARTAN Systems
➢Training	➢Word for Windows	➢Telecommunications

EXPERIENCE:

1977 to 1997

COLUMBIA PETROLEUM ENTERPRISES, INC., Cleveland, Ohio

System Programmer   **(1990-1997)**

Reported to Manager, Transaction Processing. Responsible for working with vendors and technical staff in updating system. Supervised three employees.

- Researched and identified mainframe as source of double billing error.
- Compiled, tested and modified programs. Developed test data while troubleshooting problems.
- Reduced two days of processing of customer payments by automating a manual system.
- Participated in 50 system and job installations and prepared documentation for operations, policies and procedures for each one.
- Produced JCL to correspond with specifications needed for transmissions to IBM mainframe.

Expeditor/TARTAN System   **(1987-1990)**

Reported to Supervisor. Responsible for ensuring maximum utilization of all computer facility resources to effectively meet all scheduled commitments.

- Attended and participated in walk-through during various program developments.
- Interpreted system/program specifications into program-coded instructions using TARTAN language.
- Formatted, organized and delivered several custom reports to various user groups.
- Trained both new and existing personnel on daily operation of system.

Senior Date Terminal Balancer   (1985-1987)

Reported to Supervisor. Responsible for transmission of customer cash payments and gas station transactions.

- Eliminated need for sales data submission and eight hours of staff time in accounts receivable by modifying program to accept date from another field.
- Operated TARTAN terminal system, processing transactions through electronic transmission.
- Transmitted customer credit card billing information to Visa and Discover via modems.

Computer Operator   (1985)

Responsible for processing customer payments to credit card sales.

- Operated NIXDORF 8890 mainframe.
- Maintained heat oil teleprocessing C.A.S. system.
- Scheduled nightly job batch processing.

Merchandise Clerk/Data Terminal Balancer   (1984-1985)

Senior Credit Control Clerk   (1981-1984)

Credit Control Clerk   (1980-1981)

Credit Card Authorization Clerk   (1977-1980)

EDUCATION: Baldwin-Wallace College, Berea, Ohio
Master of Business Administration
Will complete in summer of 1997

Malone College, Canton, Ohio
Bachelor of Arts in Business Management, 1994

Institute of Computer Management, Cleveland, Ohio
Certificate in Computer Languages and Programming, 1977

PROFESSIONAL DEVELOPMENT: *Career Development* seminar, Columbia Petroleum, 1996

Project Management seminar, Cleveland State University, 1996

AWARDS: Recognized for 14 years of perfect attendance

CIVIC INVOLVEMENT: Member of Photography Club

Power Resume Tip

Your resume should *never* be handwritten, written in calligraphy, duplicated by carbon paper, copied on a Ditto machine or mimeographed.

Often, Rules Are Meant *Not* to Be Broken

A By-the-Book Resume That Does Its Job Well

"No company ever hired a resume," says Robert W. Caldwell, Jr. "But your resume is important. It is a marketing piece that opens doors to the interview process."

Caldwell, the founder and president of RW Caldwell Associates, Inc., an outplacement firm, says that Marcus Grant's resume is good because it answers the three questions all resumes should answer: What do you want to do (objective)? What qualifies you to do it (summary)? How well did you do it in the past (experience and accomplishments)?

The no-nonsense Caldwell argues that an objective is necessary because "it says that you *know* what you want to do and are decisive enough to say so. It saves the reader the task of deciding for you." For instance, Marcus' objective is specific but broad enough to attract opportunities.

Caldwell explains that the summary is the resume's "hook" which could help it get more than 30 seconds of the reader's time. "In Marcus Grant's summary, note the statement 'profit center responsibility.' That's an attention-getter, the 'hook' that will elicit more than a 30-second reading."

While many recruiters advise against including personal data, Caldwell favors it when it does not sacrifice more important data because it adds "a human touch to an otherwise sterile document."

Robert Caldwell
President, RW Caldwell Associates, Inc.
Partner/Owner, Career Partners International, Ltd.*

Robert Caldwell is founder and president of RW Caldwell Associates, Inc., the oldest full-service, corporate-sponsored outplacement firm in western N.Y. The firm avoids "formula" outplacement programs. Rather, each candidate's program is developed and delivered giving personal consideration to the uniqueness of the individual involved. Those individuals include hourly employees through corporate presidents/CEOs from more than 100 client companies.

CPI has more than 130 career management services offices worldwide.

MARCUS M. GRANT

678 East River Road
Grand Island, New York 14072
Residence: (716) 555-5555
Office: (716) 853-7600

OBJECTIVE   SENIOR MANUFACTURING EXECUTIVE

SUMMARY   Progressive management experience in manufacturing, logistics/distribution, materials management, acquisitions, and business/strategic planning. Have held profit center responsibility for several turnaround business units. Skilled in re-engineering, progressive quality processes, and team building.

EXPERIENCE AND ACCOMPLISHMENTS

1987 - 1996   **WESTIN MANUFACTURING**, Buffalo, New York
Manufacturer of an extensive line of masking, cellophane, electrical, cloth, and other pressure-sensitive tape products for business, industrial, and household use.

Senior Vice President - Operations   1990 - 1996
Senior corporate manufacturing manager responsible for eight plants generating a total of $160 million in sales. Ancillary responsibility for six subsidiary plants totalling $90 million in sales. Responsible for distribution, transportation, and logistics for the corporation.

Member of the corporate strategic planning team; implemented manufacturing segments of profit center strategic and business plans. Responsible for the planning and logistics of production from plants through distribution. Analyzed acquisition targets and subsequently incorporated manufacturing operations of successful acquisitions into the company.

Managed the Corporate Engineering department with annual plant and equipment capital expenditures of $8 million. Profit center responsibility for several small, turn around business units ranging from $4 million to $15 million in sales.

Selected Accomplishments:

- Implemented process improvements that held unit distribution and manufacturing costs constant during an eight year period of flat and declining volume.
- Increased plant utilization by closing and consolidating four plants in the past six years.
- Directed the company's manufacturing re-engineering program, achieving $6 million in annual savings.
- Implemented a direct product deployment system from manufacturing to customers.
- Instituted employee involvement activities, neutralizing difficult union issues; efforts became the foundation for a team-based corporate quality improvement program.
- Consolidated the company's computer system across all manufacturing, distribution, and planning functions. Selected vendor and implemented conversion.
- Served on a team that developed and implemented an activity-based cost system.

Vice President - Manufacturing   1987 - 1990
Directed the operation of five plants with annual sales of $91 million. Oversaw production activities of five plant managers and corporate staff engaged in purchasing,transportation, engineering, environmental affairs, safety, cost accounting, and human resources.

1980 - 1987   **JAMESTOWN CHEMICAL COMPANY**, Jamestown, New York

Manufacturing Manager   1984 - 1987
Oversaw production activities of three plants engaged in the manufacture of chemical coatings, resins, gasoline additives, synthetic lubricants, catalysts, and specialty chemicals. Responsible for eight direct reports and 300 plant employees in a union environment.

Plant Manager   1980 - 1984
Responsible for two chemical coatings, resin, and specialty chemical manufacturing plants.

1973 - 1980   **PROCTER & GAMBLE**, Chicago, Illinois

Assistant Plant Manager   1975 - 1980
Quality Assurance Manager   1973 - 1975

EDUCATION   M.B.A;, Manufacturing Concentration, 1973
Northwestern University, Evanston, Illinois

B.S. Chemical Engineering, with honors, 1971
Worcester Polytechnic Institute, Worcester, MA

PERSONAL   Married with three grown children; active in competitive sports; excellent health.

Power Resume Tip

When your resume is completely finished, don't make a single mark on it. Don't pencil in a note, write in an updated phone number or try to cover up an error with correction fluid. The resume you send out must be absolutely flawless.

The Value of Good, Clear Writing

The 'Write' Resume Will Stand Out from the Crowd

So few people know how to write well these days that a well-turned phrase in a resume can turn employers' heads.

"Individuals conducting a job search often think of their resume as a simple summary of their professional work history," say Melinda A. Schneider and Richard E. Widuch, partners in Schneider Widuch in Pasadena, Calif. "However, many employers also use the resume to evaluate a person's communications abilities. A well-written resume always will stand out from the crowd."

Susan O'Shear's resume certainly supports that view. Scanning it, the reader comes away with the impression that the candidate can communicate *clearly*. While one might quibble with some of O'Shear's choices of words, her resume certainly conveys that this candidate "has accomplished specific events each year with important results," say Schneider/Widuch.

The consultants point out that the five keys to success in producing effective resumes are "personality, style, content, implementation and impact." The latter three are the areas the candidate must focus on in producing the resume—job responsibilities, what was accomplished in each of those positions and what effects those achievements had.

While doing this, the candidate must also be careful to allow his or her personality to come through. Note at the bottom of the first page of O'Shear's resume, she discusses her management of a downsizing, careful to emphasize that she spent at least 45 minutes with each of the laid-off employees. O'Shear thus portrays herself as a disciplined *and* concerned manager.

"The style should provide a sense of the human being behind the words," say Schneider/Widuch. "This approach can cause companies to conclude that you should be hired because the firm will be better off."

Melinda A. Schneider and Richard E. Widuch
Partners, Schneider Widuch

Schneider Widuch, established in 1983, is an outplacement firm dedicated to assisting management and individuals achieve their business and career goals. The firm is particularly successful with those individuals having strong personalities and those who need sensitive, caring guidance and confidence enhancement. Each participant's program is uniquely developed and delivered based on the personal and career needs of the individual. The firm does not use any type of "canned" outplacement program. Schneider Widuch is a member of the Association of Outplacement Consulting Firms International (AOCFI).

SUSAN A. O'SHEAR
925 Palm Drive
Glendale, California 91202
Telephone: (818) 555-1992

SUMMARY

A successful cross-industry experienced Senior Human Resources professional with a proven track record in dynamic business environments.

SELECTED ACHIEVEMENTS

- Managed the merger integration process in Los Angeles on behalf of Bank of America Corporate Services Group located in San Francisco and Security Pacific Corporation through intensive one-on-one meetings with affected employees explaining rights, options, and all aspects of the Merger Transition Program during a two month period.

- Managed the elimination of the Corporate Aviation Department, including business case development and analysis, employee separations and the transfer of operations to alternative service providers, which saved the Corporation more than $2.6 million.

- Managed the staffing strategy for the Gibraltar acquisition to ensure that key employees were retained during the conversion of treasury and finance operations.

- Designed and implemented with executive management a performance evaluation system targeted towards corporate financial managers and professional staff.

- Created a "Mentor Program" for minority corporate officers. The program was implemented under the direction of the Multi-Cultural Officers Network organization.

PROFESSIONAL EXPERIENCE

BANK OF AMERICA, Los Angeles, CA — 1992

Vice President, Manager, Merger Integration — Los Angeles, Executive Staff

Reported to Vice President, Corporate Services Group. Responsible for managing the merger integration process between Security Pacific Corporation and Bank of America. The process involved intensive meetings and discussions with affected employees; planning and implementation of strategies to retain essential staff and to reduce staff where necessary to ensure the profitability goals of the merger. Directly eliminated 211 employees through intensive one-on-one meetings with each meeting lasting between 45 minutes to several hours during the 60 day period. Developed the Senior Vice President and above displacement plan and was responsible for unit close down and securing assets.

SECURITY PACIFIC CORPORATION, Los Angeles, CA 1983 — 1992

Vice President, Senior Human Resources Consultant, 1986 — 1992

Reported to Senior Vice President, Human Resources Services, and served a client base of over 800 executives, managers and professionals. Responsibilities included Employee Relations with accountability for implementing, communicating and interpreting policies, programs and legal issues, resolution of grievances, and reduction-in-force business case implementation; Employment and Management Recruiting with accountability for development and execution of recruiting strategies, staffing and organizational analysis and career transition counseling; Management Development with accountability for assessing developmental needs and providing programs to increase professional growth and maximize productivity; and Compensation with responsibility for developing job evaluations, job family descriptions, career path models and succession plans in support of retention strategy and expense control targets.

Vice President, Manager, Management Development 1983 — 1986

Reported to Senior Vice President, Human Resources. Directly responsible for a Division that provided supervisory and management skills training to the Corporation. Managed the Educational Assistance, Career Management and New Employee Orientation programs. Annual operating budget of $2.1 million and 14 professional training staff members. Previous assignments were Manager, Training Operations and Senior Program Designer.

TECHNICOLOR, INC., Los Angeles, CA 1982 — 1983

National Training Director

Reported to Vice President, Operations. Responsible for the creation and startup of the training function for a new subsidiary. Created "Technicolor Tech", a multi-week training program encompassing personnel policy and administration, financial management, sales and customer service training and technical areas. Wrote and published company operating manual with line management.

ORANGE JULIUS OF AMERICA, Santa Monica, CA 1978 — 1982

National Training Director

Reported to Vice President, Operations. Responsible for the creation of "Orange Julius University", an intensive business management training program for new franchisees. Previous assignments were Western Regional Training Manager and National Communications Director.

EDUCATION

UCLA, Los Angeles, CA, B.A. Degree
        Continuing education: Advanced Program for Human Resources Executives, University of
        Michigan; Advanced Conference on Labor Relations Law, IAML; Organizational Consulting
        Program, Skopos.

RELATED ACTIVITIES

        Personnel Policy Committee, San Fernando Valley Girl Scout Council.
        Society for Human Resource Management.
        Adviser, Multi-Cultural Officers Network, Security Pacific Corporation.
        Founding Member, Security Pacific's SpeakersBank, a volunteer organization providing public
        speakers to professional and nonprofit community organizations.

Power Resume Tip

When detailing current positions, use the present tense. When describing previous experiences, use past tense. Also, use short phrases, and leave out unnecessary articles, such as "I," "the," "an," etc.

Stick to the Point and You'll Make Points

Never Burden the Resume Reader

"A good resume must be short and get right to the point," stresses Robert Greenberg, president of Scientific Search in Mt. Laurel, N.J. "I give each resume only 30 seconds to convince me the candidate has the experience I'm looking for. All the information I want to know should be smack in front of my eyes."

The recruiter especially likes Craig's resume because:

Craig's educational background is presented right away, confirming that he possesses a technical degree from a good school. Greenberg doesn't have to scan to the bottom of the page in search of academic credentials.

From a technical standpoint, the next three sections provide an information technology recruiter with the most important information he needs: the computer languages, assemblers and operating systems the candidate knows. "These three items, listed right away, give me an immediate picture of Craig's skills," Greenberg says. "They are critical and therefore appear on their own, rather than buried in sentences under Work Experience."

The Work Experience section tells the recruiter that Craig has worked with well-established companies over decent periods of time. When reviewing job responsibilities, Greenberg tends to look at the first three words in each line, scanning for signs that the candidate is a do-er. In Craig's resume, the recruiter finds what he's looking for: "designed and implemented," "supervised," "designed and coded" and "worked with clients."

"A resume should never be burdensome to the person who has to review it," says Greenberg. "Stick to the point and your resume will get the attention it deserves."

Robert Greenberg
President, Scientific Search, Inc.

In 1983, Robert Greenberg started Scientific Search, a Mt. Laurel, New Jersey-based search firm which fills information technology positions in every type of organization. Prior to that, he spent 14 years in the data processing profession.

Craig T. Wilson
330 Brookside Drive
Mt. Laurel, NJ 08054
609-555-1234

EDUCATION

B.S. Computer Science (3.0/4.0) with minor in Electrical Engineering
Pennsylvania State University, graduated 1986

LANGUAGES

C, COBOL, Visual BASIC, Oracle, Pascal, PL/a, Ada

ASSEMBLERS

80x86, 6502, IBM 370

OPERATING SYSTEMS

UNIX, Windows, DOS, VM/CMA, MVS/XA, OS/2

WORK EXPERIENCE

<u>Programmer Analyst</u>   Company A
May 1994 to present   Mt. Laurel, NJ

- lead programmer on project to reengineer sales order system
- designed and implemented systems utilizing EID and IVR enabling technologies
- worked closely with clients to establish problem specifications and system designs
- supervised two contract programmers

<u>Programmer Analyst</u>   Company B
September 1990 to May 1994   Philadelphia, PA

- lead programmer on two corporate projects to upgrade segments of claims and premium processing systems
- developed and implemented several enhancements to worker's compensation and commercial auto systems
- designed and coded systems to upload date from PC-based policy rating system to mainframe-based data entry screens

<u>Programmer</u>   Company C
full time: August 1986 to September 1990   Mt. Laurel, NJ
part time: June 1983 to July 1986

- part of team that designed and implemented a custom accounting system
- developed and implemented disaster recovery plan
- supervised one programmer

<u>Electronic Technician</u>   Company D
part time: January 1980 to December 1982   Moorestown, NJ

- assembled and tested microcontroller-based control systems
- verified design revisions and component layouts

REFERENCES   available upon request

A Resume to Open Doors

Present Qualifications So That Companies Can Find Them

"Michelle earned interviews with three of the eight companies she wanted to reach," says Craig L. VanKouwenberg, executive recruiter and Certified Career Development Consultant. "This is truly a resume to open doors."

Although she doesn't have an undergraduate degree, Michelle also managed to increase her annual income $20,000. In addition, she changed industry groups. Extraordinary results!

Why? VanKouwenberg points out that Michelle's resume is easy to read and easy to understand. In her common sense, chronological format, she shows significant accomplishments and concern for people.

"She also reveals results from luck, much hard work, superior intelligence and outstanding people skills," says VanKouwenberg, whose business is in Lancaster, Pa. "She shows how she overcame adversity and kept up-to-date with both emerging management techniques and industry-related manufacturing technologies."

He adds that Michelle discovered a shared consistency among the companies who wanted to interview her:

- Her interest in work force development.

- Her demonstrated abilities as a strong, people-oriented manager able to handle both the bigger picture and the smaller details.

- Her through-the-ranks promotions.

- Most of all, her results.

"Her resume presented her qualifications well, and the companies found them," says the recruiter.

Craig L. VanKouwenberg
Search and Recruitment

Craig L. VanKouwenberg, executive recruiter and Certified Career Development Consultant, accomplished his doctoral studies at Princeton Theological Seminary. He began his formal work in the employment field as an army chaplain during the Vietnam era.

VanKouwenberg designed and developed the first (Pennsylvania) state-approved training program in outplacement and career development. He also has served as a resource consultant for Joyce Lain Kennedy's national *Careers* column, for psychologists and other professionals working in the employment services industry, and for government and university employment transition programs. He can be reached via voice mail at 717-293-9696.

Michelle K. Frasier
1210 Morningside Drive
Lancaster, PA 17603
717-555-0000

SUMMARY: Fully capable in developing and motivating personnel to achieve World Class and competitive performance objectives. Strong management skills in both vertical and team oriented organizations. Demonstrated expertise in:

- *Operations*
- *Organization and Planning*
- *Cost Reductions*
- *Quality Control*
- *Personnel Training, OSHA, Environmental Compliance*
- *Process Control & Continuous Improvement*

PROFESSIONAL HISTORY

1994—Present   Master Technologies, Inc., Lancaster, PA

Promoted to Director of Manufacturing Operations	*Sept. 94—Present*
Manager, Manufacturing Operations & Development	*Apr. 94—Sept. 94*
Production Manager	*Jan. 94—Apr. 94*

Responsible for providing strategic and tactical direction for improvements in Process Engineering, Industrial Engineering, Production and Training departments for company of 250 employees at 60MM/year in the design, manufacturing and sales of PC communications equipment. Responsibilities and accomplishments include, but not limited to:

- Successful facilitation and management of growth at 10X in one year.
    ◊ Justification and installation of 3MM in capital equipment.
    ◊ Improved quality from 85% to yields above 97%.
    ◊ Reduced scrap to less than .3%.
    ◊ Reduced equipment change over time to .5 hours, from more than 3 hours.
    ◊ Reduced cost by increases in efficiency up to 25%.
- Met ISO9000 Quality system standards through coordinating company-wide training, education and documentation.
- Used automated MRPII system for operations planning, including master scheduling and product costing.
- Implemented change and configuration control procedures to improve standard specifications for product build and design for manufacturing.
- Reduced cost of workforce development through design and implementation of screening and testing process for new hires.
- Utilized up to 75K/year of state granted funds to offset training costs.
- Developed curriculum and facilitated company training for "Train the Trainer", "Employee Development", "SPC", "Leadership Training" and "Workmanship Standards".

1990—92   The "K" Corporation, Downers Grove, IL
    Promoted to Project Manager, Process Engineering   ***Sept. 91—Dec. 92***
    Process Engineering Support   ***July 90—Sept. 91***

Improved quality, reduced costs for manufacturing job shop.
- Handled engineering, production, purchasing, sales and customer satisfaction issues for 300 employees at $13MM+/year firm.
    ◊ Commended for work on AT&T project, providing project leadership.
- Developed, maintained and documented product manufacturing processes.
    ◊ Reduced costs by 10% by creating and releasing accurate and complete specifications for product build.
    ◊ Corrected severe SPC training, operating procedure and documentation problems to secure recertification from Caterpillar Corporation—and their designation as a Top Supplier.

1980—89   IBM Corporation, Tucson, AZ
    Promoted from Machine Operator to Department Technician, to Production Control to Product Analyst (with Planning responsibilities) to Manufacturing Manager.

- Directly coordinated with and/or held responsibilities in all manufacturing and test areas.
- Responsible for personnel and production management.
- OSHA, training and safety requirements handled in addition to personnel performance plans and evaluations.
    ◊ Reduced defects 97%, cycle time 45% and inventory 60%.

1980   AGM Electronics, Tucson, AZ
    Production Worker

1978—80   Pennsylvania Scale Company, Leola, PA
    Production Worker

EDUCATION

1994   Penn State University, Lancaster Campus
    Course work towards A.P.I.C.S. PCIM Certification

1986—1989   University of Arizona & Pima Community College, Tucson, AZ
    Course work in Electronics, Algebra, Management, Sciences & the Humanities

    Nearly 450 class hours of graduate level training in Management, Supervision, Personnel and technical areas including MRP, MRPII, JIT and World Class Manufacturing.

AWARDS AND RECOGNITION

More than a dozen events of employer awards and formal recognitions.

EXCELLENT REFERENCES AVAILABLE

Power Resume Tip

If you've had little or no work experience or are returning to the job market after an absence, be sure to include any volunteer experience, social responsibilities or charitable activities on your resume. Employers are interested in people who are "doers," regardless of monetary compensation.

A Resume That Answers
Most Employers' Questions

Clear and Specific Information

No one would ever accuse Kathryn Johnson, whose resume appears over the following four pages, of being an underachiever.

This resume is "incredibly clear and specific," says Barbara L. Provus, the principal and cofounder of Shepherd Bueschel & Provus, Inc.

"Putting the position titles in boldface all-caps ensures that they jump out at you. She provides brief descriptions of the companies, and defines reporting and staff relationships so that the resume reviewer will have a clear idea of her career track and the types of environments in which she worked."

In addition, Johnson lists her accomplishments and responsibilities, keeping the explanations very brief so that they can be easily scanned.

"Kathryn also demonstrates that she was active in—not just a member of—ap-propriate professional organizations," says Provus.

"There's plenty of data here, but it's all relevant and would definitely be sufficient to determine the individual's technical qualifications for a position."

However, despite her admiration for this resume, Provus has some reservations about it. "I think that it could be a little shorter, particularly if Kathryn had condensed her earlier work experience. I would also suggest the inclusion of information on her professional objectives, ability to relocate, etc. In addition, since this is such a long resume, a summary would have helped ensure that the important information gets noticed."

Barbara Provus
Principal, Cofounder, Shepherd Bueschel & Provus, Inc.

Shepherd Bueschel & Provus, Inc., develops and conducts senior-level executive search assignments for a wide range of major U.S. and multinational corporations.

Previously, Provus was a vice president with a "top ten" international executive search firm; manager of Management Development for Federated Department Stores; and held several positions in human resources and executive search with Booz, Allen & Hamilton.

Provus is active in several professional and nonprofit associations.

KATHRYN J. JOHNSON
1234 James Street, Chicago, Illinois 60000
(312) 555-4567 (residence)
(312) 555-4321 (business)

EDUCATION

Purdue University, Lafayette, Indiana, B.A., Political Science, 1974, Summa Cum Laude

University of Michigan, Ann Arbor, Michigan, M.A., Library Science, 1978; M.B.A., 1987, Marketing Concentration

EMPLOYMENT HISTORY

GARFIELD CORPORATION
Chicago, Illinois
July 1993 to Present

Garfield Corporation is a manufacturer and distributor of food ingredients. The company serves its 3,000 customers through a network of six plants located throughout the United States. For Fiscal Year 1995, sales were approximately $400 million, with approximately 2,000 employees. The company's common stock is listed and traded on the American Stock Exchange.

VICE PRESIDENT, PUBLIC AFFAIRS

Reports to Chairman and Chief Executive Officer.
No staff.
Responsible for creating, implementing and managing overall corporate communications programs. Develops strategy for ongoing communications with investors, the media and employees designed to present the company's strategies, prospects and activities to its various constituencies:

Investor Relations

—Maintains contact with security analysts, portfolio managers and security holders.
—Writes, edits and produces annual and quarterly reports to shareholders.
—Arranges and manages meetings with financial community.
—Manages annual meeting; writes speeches for management.

Media Relations

—Writes and distributes press releases including quarterly and annual earnings announcements, personnel announcements and new product introductions.
—Handles all media inquiries; arranges interviews with management.
—Serves as company spokesman with financial and trade media.

Employee Communications

—Writes, edits and produces quarterly employee newsletter.
—Arranges all employee meetings; prepares remarks for management.

Public Relations

—Writes, edits and produces corporate marketing materials.
—Advises management on public relations activities.
—Writes speeches for and provides communications counsel to management.

Developed overall corporate communications strategy. Brought "in-house" investor relations and media relations activities previously handled by outside consultants. Resulted in annual savings of $200,000.

Developed and instituted quarterly employee newsletter.

Wrote, edited and produced first corporate marketing brochure.

Wrote executive speeches for analyst meetings, all employee meetings, paper industry conferences and community, industrial and development meetings.

Developed guidelines and program for corporate contributions.

Wrote, edited and produced marketing brochure on company's recycled products.

CRANSCO FOODS   DIRECTOR, INVESTOR RELATIONS
February 1991 to June 1993   Boise, Idaho

Cransco Foods manufacturers grocery products including cheese, pourable dressings for salads, mayonnaise and salad dressing, barbeque sauce, margarine, condiments, confections and fruit spreads. Annual sales for Cransco were approximately $4.8 billion in 1992, with 12,000 employees. Cransco was acquired by Miller Corp. 1993, at which point the Director, Investor Relations position was eliminated at Cransco.

Reported to the Vice President of Investor Relations.

Managed two support staff.

Responsible for developing and implementing investor relations programs directed toward institutional investors.

Maintained ongoing communications with analysts and portfolio managers in the U.S. and Europe.

Wrote speeches, developed multimedia presentations and prepared financial press releases.

Analyzed peer group and industry data, prepared reports and recommendations to management on investor-related issues and monitored trading activity and share ownership in the U.S., Europe and Japan.

Headed task force formed to advise management on how to increase employee ownership of Cransco stock through modification of the company's thrift plan.

Managed two-day seminar for 100 security analysts and financial media at which Cransco's most senior executives made presentations.

Responsibilities included program theme and content, speech and slide preparation, production of collateral pieces and logistics.

Served on task force responsible for successfully listing Cransco stock on the Tokyo Stock Exchange; negotiated fees and services with dividend paying agent.

Implemented new procedures for dissemination of information to security analysts resulting in annual savings of $10,000.

Updated the investor relations department computer systems resulting in annual savings of $24,000.

MWJ CORPORATION
Denver, Colorado
October 1983 to January 1991

MJW Corporation was a natural resources (oil and gas) company with annual revenues of approximately $900 million.

September 1984 to January 1991   **DIRECTOR, FINANCIAL RELATIONS**

October 1983 to August 1984   **ASSISTANT DIRECTOR, FINANCIAL RELATIONS**

Reported to the Chairman and CEO.

Managed staff of two.

Responsible for creating, implementing and managing communications programs directed toward investors, the media and employees for this $2 billion independent oil and gas company.

Wrote, edited and produced annual and quarterly reports to shareholders.

Maintained contact with security analysts and portfolio managers, wrote speeches and prepared slide presentations.

Served as company spokesman with national and local media and the financial community.

Provided communications counsel to management.

Managed investor and media relations during crisis situations, including well explosions, lawsuits, unusual stock trading activity, proxy fights, financial restructurings and tender offers.

Initiated Investor Reference Guide to explain complicated corporate structure and Company's capabilities to security analysts; initiated Corporate Fact Book as a quick reference for financial and operational statistics.

Received Nicholson Award for Best in Industry Annual Report from National Association of Investors Corporation.

UNITED STATES SENATE
United States Federal Government
Springfield, Illinois
January 1978 to September 1983

November 1979 to September 1983   **STAFF AIDE TO U.S. SENATOR JOHN DOE**

Responsible for scheduling the Senator's activities.

Prepared agendas, speeches, constituent profiles, background and briefing materials; organized media coverage and press releases.

Coordinated the Senator's nominations to military academies.

Performed constituent casework and special project analysis covering Department of State, Justice and HEW.

January 1978 to October 1979   **STAFF ASSISTANT**

Prepared financial reports filed with Federal Election Commission and Secretary of the Senate for Doe for Senate Campaign Committee.

UNIVERSITY OF KANSAS　　　　　　　　　　**LIBRARIAN**
February 1973 to January 1978　　　　　　　　Lawrence, Kansas

   Served as liaison for the University library and 1,500 foreign and domestic book dealers.

   Responsible for resolving problems with book orders, monitoring $3 million book budget, authorizing invoice payments, preparing annual acquisition statistics.

PROFESSIONAL AFFILIATIONS

Food Industry Finance Exchange, 1992 to Present

National Investor Relations Institute
   Board of Directors, 1988 to 1992
   Vice President/Secretary, 1991 to 1992
   Vice President/Strategic Planning, 1990 to 1991
   Vice President/Membership, 1989 to 1990

Public Relations Society of America, 1984 to 1991

Power Resume Tip

Avoid including personal statistics, hobbies or outside interests on your resume. This information is usually irrelevant and may even bias a potential employer against you.

Don't Tell Me, Sell Me

A Powerful, Accomplishment-Driven Resume

Your resume needs to show prospective employers what you're responsible for on the job, but don't do it with a long laundry list of job duties, says Marie Keenen Mansheim, president of Summit Career Services.

"Use a list of accomplishments instead," says the Visalia, California-based career coach. "Employers are looking to solve problems. They'll judge your ability to solve their problems by what you have achieved in the past."

Mansheim advises when listing accomplishments that you *quantify* your results. Think about what you've achieved and be *specific*.

"For example, showing sales increases as percentages will take the mystery out of the numbers," she says.

John Christianson's resume is just such an example. John is ready for a change, not in his career, but in his location. He'd like to move across the country but maintain his position in the beverage industry, where he's successfully advanced throughout his professional life. John includes a paragraph about his job responsibilities—making good use of specific information—and then details his accomplishments in a separate section.

"As in John's resume, don't be afraid to use industry jargon," Mansheim says. "Using key words and the technical jargon of your industry will paint a picture of you as an insider."

She adds that a summary of your background can be the most difficult part of the resume-writing process. You need to show who you are, what your strengths are and what you can do for the prospective employer. Note how John does that by highlighting his skills and achievements in a power-packed overview.

Marie Keenen Mansheim
Owner/President, Summit Career Services

Marie Keenen Mansheim is a professional resume writer and career coach who has advised clients nationwide since 1992 in all aspects of resume writing and career management. She possesses a wide range of sales, marketing and human resources skills, backed by a marketing degree and sales and executive recruiting experience.

Mansheim is an accomplished public speaker on resume writing, job-search planning and career marketing/management issues. She also is a featured columnist for the Professional Association of Resume Writers monthly newsletter.

JOHN CHRISTIANSON

3343 Orchard Court
Visalia, California
Home: (209) 555-0703
Work: (209) 555-0709

SENIOR SALES & MANAGEMENT PROFESSIONAL

Dynamic management career marketing and selling beverage products within a competitive business market. Expert in building top-producing sales organizations through strategic marketing, tactical sales, and key account management. Outstanding record of achievement in account and contract negotiations. Excellent communicator coupled with an ability to actively manage change. Demonstrated achievements in:

- Key Account Relationship Management
- Strategic Sales and Market Planning
- Competitive New Product Launch

- Sales Training & Development
- Regional Budgeting & Forecasting
- Pricing & Service Management

Computer Skills: Norand, Margin Minder, Windows, Lotus, WordPerfect, Power Point, and Microsoft Office Works

---

EXPERIENCE

SUPERIOR NO-NAME BEVERAGE COMPANY, Visalia, CA   1972-Present
Sales Manager, 1985-Present
(Distributor with sales of $2 million in a four county area with a total population of 275,000)

Manage Eagle and Tulare counties with a total of 900 customer accounts. Track and manage sales margins by account, driver, and brand on a daily basis for the 50 largest accounts. Assign sales and revenue goals for the two county area, two route managers, and seven route drivers. Develop, budget, and implement marketing programs and administer a quarter of a million dollars in the SCA program. Budget for and order $120,000 of new vending machines per year. Administer co-op budget of $15,000 per year and purchase all POS materials. Train route drivers and coordinate driver and truck compliance with DOT, federal, and state transportation regulations. Write reviews for all direct reports and a member of a three-person employment team.

<u>Accomplishments:</u>

- Developed and implemented a series of cost reduction/cost avoidance programs.
- Initiated a telesell presell program for customers buying less than 10 cases per week.
- Reconfigured the delivery fleet from 25 to 24 trucks through a series of bodystyling and routing changes.
- Personally orchestrated the acquisition of a new vending account with an initial order volume of 30,000 cases per year.
- Achieved an average of 7% over quota since becoming Sales Manager.
- Member of two regionalized Joint Account Call Teams (JACT), consisting of myself, a bottling representative, and a No-Name Beverage Company representative. Personally brought 120 independently-owned convenience stores on board as a chain account.
- Chairman of the California Retailer Committee of the CA Beverage Bottlers Association.

ADDITIONAL EXPERIENCE

SUPERIOR NO-NAME BEVERAGE COMPANY, Visalia, CA
Food Service Sales/Service, 1980-1985
Vending Sales/Service, 1975-1978
Route Driver, 1972-1975

EDUCATION

No-Name Beverage Company Corporation Sales Training Programs, 1975-Present
Dale Carnegie Course - 1991
Riverbend Technical College, Fundamentals of Marketing - 1982
Mead Computer Training - Lotus, Windows, and WordPerfect Courses
Licensed Tractor Trailer CDL

PROFESSIONAL AFFILIATIONS

California Grocers Association, Member
Visalia Chamber of Commerce - Chairman of Industrial Park Committee
Tulare Chamber of Commerce, Member
Private School, Volunteer - Alumni and Student Fundraising

References Available Upon Request

Power Resume Tip

Use bullets or asterisks to highlight accomplishments or explanatory phrases. This not only breaks up a lot of information into bite-size portions, but also helps pull out key selling points that would be buried if presented in long paragraph form.

"Downsized" Out of a Job May
Mean "Downsizing" Your Resume

Even the Highly Experienced Can Have One-Page Resumes

When his subsidiary was divested, David Dow, a 30-year veteran of the work force, suddenly found himself out of a job. Candidates with this much experience often write three- or four-page resumes, reports The Swain Consulting Group co-founder Robert Swain. However, David knew that in this tough employment climate it's best to make your resume easily readable.

"An easy scan of this resume should tell the reader just enough to decide whether the experience and credentials are appropriate for a prospective opening," says Swain, co-author of *Out the Organization*. "The task of presenting a long record of experience runs headlong into the limited attention span of resume readers. In fact, we doubt that resumes are ever *read*—believing that most are merely scanned."

Particularly strong is the Background Summary, which provides two concise sentences and six points making the candidate's areas of expertise stand out clearly.

This resume shoots down the claim of so many candidates that they "can't fit everything" onto one page.

Robert Swain
Founder, The Swain Consulting Group

Robert Swain is founder and co-chair of The Swain Consulting Group, an organizational development firm in New York specializing in senior management coaching. Swain is co-author of *Out the Organization*, now in its third printing by Master Media.

DAVID DOW
596 Overlook Avenue
New York, NY 10031
212-555-6543

BACKGROUND SUMMARY

GENERAL MANAGER with extensive experience in marketing and sales, operations, R&D and the financial management of medium and high-tech businesses. Product knowledge spans lasers & optronics, telecommunications, energy, industrial products and computer services. Related areas of expertise are:

Market Development	Quality Control	Productivity Improvement
Product Engineering	Turnarounds	Cost Reduction Programs

EXPERIENCE

JONES/LOCKWOOD (formerly Lockwood Co.)
President, Garden City, N.Y., since 1993.
Manage this profitable $12 million subsidiary in the development, manufacturing and sale of scientific equipment to the aerospace, industrial, university, OEM, defense and export markets. Responsible for U.S. and Canadian sales and operations, R&D, finance and human resources. During last two years, sales have increased 20% in a depressed market, while profits rose from a loss of $1.5 million to a positive contribution of $1 million. Significantly upgraded engineering and office support computer systems and software. Company recently acquired from French parent by Jones Corporation, a U.S. company.

XYZ CORPORATION.
Director, North American Marketing & Sales, XYZ Belgium, 1987 to 1993
Based in New Jersey, developed and directed North American sales office, achieving substantial growth in the export distribution of sophisticated electronic control devices. Built solid customer base, contributed 50% of company's total income and expanded established product lines with new technologies.

Director, Operations, XYZ Belgium, 1983 to 1987
Based in the Hague with P&L and turnaround responsibility for 950 employees, multi-plant operations, producing telecommunications equipment and military electronics. Achieved profitable status through implementation of: cost reduction program, on-line computer design capability and 50% increase in factory efficiency. Unit went from $2 million annual loss to net profit of $1.5 million.

Director, Operations, XYZ Scandinavia, 1981 to 1983.
Based in Copenhagen with responsibility for operations of five companies with sales of +$500 million. Planned and implemented expansion programs in two countries, consolidated two manufacturing operations and established highly profitable co-production facility for F-16 electronics.

Operations Executive, XYZ World Headquarters, New York, 1976 to 1981.
Developed and implemented major improvement programs at various XYZ companies worldwide, spanning telecommunications, automotive, industrial and consumer goods.

Earlier XYZ assignments included establishing new company to manufacture submarine cables and serving as assistant to Vice President, Operations, focusing on cost improvement and return on assets, 1966 to 1976.

EDUCATION

B.S.I.E., College of Mechanical Technology, Brussels.

PERSONAL

Married, two children. Multi-lingual (English, Dutch, German, French).

No Bull and Plenty of Bullets

A Resume That Dazzles the Reader with Facts

Read this resume through and see if you notice that anything is missing.

Odds are, you probably *didn't* notice that there is no section labeled Education. Why? Because Eugene D. Thompson, a highly capable candidate in most other respects, never attended college. Therefore, he omitted an Education section because "there's simply no reason to bring up a weakness," says Kenneth Newton, cofounder and principal of Transition Associates in Richmond, Va.

"In the same manner, if education is not a strength, but you still want to include it, put it *after* Experience, not right at the top," advises the career consultant.

He adds that a resume *must not* contain false information, including inaccurate dates. Any factual error may be grounds for termination of employment obtained using the false information.

"The resume is designed to *sell* the candidate, not give the employer a reason *not* to buy," Newton says. He uses this resume as an example of the "general concepts" he believes should apply to all resumes.

"It uses a Summary rather than an Objective. I believe that an objective is either so general as to be meaningless or so specific that it can exclude the writer from consideration for related positions.

"In addition, the emphasis is on accomplishments, rather than on duties. People are not hired for *what* they do as much as they are for how *well* they do it."

What's more, these accomplishments are in numeric and percentage terms. "Who would not be attracted to someone who reduced an operating budget by 11 percent or increased profitability of a subsidiary by $3.5 million in one year?"

Kenneth Newton
Cofounder, Principal, Transition Associates

Transition Associates, located in Richmond, Va., specializes in corporate outplacement and individual career consulting. Kenneth Newton's background includes a career in professional recruiting and in training in interpersonal communications. He's a charter member of the International Association of Career Management Professionals.

EUGENE D. THOMPSON
1060 Route 1
Ashland, KY 41101
H - 606-555-1234
W - 606-555-7890

SUMMARY:

A professional manager with experience in administration and technical coordination of insurance claim functions for multiple branch offices.

EXPERIENCE:

3/88 - Present

Williams Holdings, an American International Division
NATIONAL CLAIM DIRECTOR. Ashland, KY

- Responsible for supervising home office claims and four claim service offices for this excess and surplus lines insurance carrier.
- Developed and implemented the first complete corporate technical and procedures claim manual, including time and service standards for file reporting and improving the quality of service to policyholders.
- Reduced operating budget by 11%.
- Achieved a 50% reduction in outstanding cases in litigation over two years.

1962 - 1988

Commercial Insurance Company
REGIONAL CLAIM MANAGER. Harrisburg, PA (2/81 - 3/88)

- Technical and personnel responsibilities for regional claim activities and six branch claim offices in the mid-Atlantic states.
- Achieved a 60% reduction in outstanding claim files.
- Increased the income to Commercial Life Insurance, a subsidiary of Commercial Insurance Company, from $0 to $3.5 million a year by utilizing structured settlements in settlement of casualty claims.
- Reduced staffing from 165 to 118 with no adverse effect on the quality of claim service.
- Reduced the use of independent adjusters on claims from 12% to 1%.

ASSISTANT TERRITORIAL DIRECTOR, HOME OFFICE CLAIMS.
New York, NY (1979 - 81)

- Responsible for quality control program and home office audit program for 40 offices countrywide.
- Conducted an average of two home office audits in the field offices per month.

BRANCH CLAIM MANAGER. Springfield, MO (1969 - 79)

- Responsible for the management, technical claim handling and training of claim personnel to handle all lines of claims for the four counties in western Missouri.
- The youngest person to be appointed to the position of Claim Manager at the time of promotion.
- One of two persons selected from the claim department by the company countrywide to become Assistant Branch Manager in charge of underwriting and loss control functions.
- Developed five supervisors who were selected for promotion to Claim Manager in other offices.

BRANCH CLAIM SUPERVISOR. Hamden, CT (1965 - 69)

- Responsible for direct supervision and development of four adjusters handling all lines of property and casualty claims.

OUTSIDE CLAIM ADJUSTER. Hamden, CT (1962 - 65)

- Responsible for handling all lines of claims as an outside adjuster in the assigned territory.

New Hampshire Insurance Company
1960 - 1962   HOME OFFICE PROPERTY CLAIM EXAMINER. Manchester, NH

Peerless Insurance Company
1958 - 1960   JUNIOR FIRE UNDERWRITER. Keene, NH

AFFILIATIONS:

Member - Excess and Surplus Lines Claim Association
Past President - Claim Managers Council

Power Resume Tip

Make sure the typeface you select is big enough to read, but not overwhelming. The standard type size for the main text of a resume is 11 points.

Keep It Simple

What's the Purpose of Creating an Effective Resume?

In today's competitive job market, an effective resume is essential, says Beth Ann Ring, placement director at Valley College of Technology.

"A prospective employer may spend only 10 seconds glancing at your resume," she adds. "Your job is to create an 'effective resume' which will communicate convincingly your qualifications for the position. Then your resume can serve its primary purpose, which is to get you an interview."

When preparing your resume, Ring advises that you always assume the reader knows nothing about you or your qualifications. Try to collect job descriptions to use as a reference when preparing your resume. Slant your current or prior experience toward the job you're seeking and always use action words or verbs.

"An effective resume will emphasize your *accomplishments and abilities* and *secure that interview*," she concludes.

Beth Ann Ring
Placement Director, Valley College of Technology

Valley College of Technology, located in Martinsburg, W. Va., is a computer and business school that offers training to adult students and businesses in the community. Valley College is committed to the development of graduates who are proficient in occupational readiness, employability skills and technical excellence. Beth Ann Ring has more than 12 years of experience in post-secondary education and training, 10 of which have been in career counseling and placement.

SANDRA M. BOOTH
1234 Happy Trail Way
Martinsburg, WV 25401
(304) 123-4567

OBJECTIVE

To obtain a secretarial/receptionist position where I can utilize my computer and clerical skills.

PROFESSIONAL SKILLS

- MS DOS
- Windows
- dBase III
- Lotus 1-2-3
- WordPerfect 5.1/6.1

- Filing/Editing
- Typing (55+ wpm)
- Office Procedures
- Telephone Skills
- SuperWrite (80 wpm)

- Accounting
- Business Math
- Business English
- Management Skills
- Customer Service Skills

EDUCATION

Office Technology Program / **Secretarial Specialty**
Valley College of Technology, Martinsburg WV, Completion Date: 6/97
G.P.A. 3.9/4.0; Attendance 100%

EMPLOYMENT SKILLS

- Developed ability to work in a fast pace atmosphere
- Maintained excellent customer relations and developed customer rapport
- Diplomatically resolved customers complaints on as needed basis
- Accurately calculated and made daily deposits up to $20,000
- Ability to follow instructions well and make decisions with no supervision
- Motivated and supervised 15+ employees on daily basis
- Maintained all record keeping procedures without error
- Delegated responsibilities to employees to meet company's expectations
- Effectively developed telephone communication skills and consistently met quotas

EMPLOYMENT HISTORY

Assistant Manager, Roger's Fuel Center, Hagerstown, MD	06/95 - 11/97
Telemarketer, DEF Group, Martinsburg, WV, Temporary Assignment	06/94 - 12/94
Data Entry Operator, AMI, Martinsburg, WV, James Rumsey Internship	December 1993

A "Magic" Resume That's a Three-Time Winner

Built for the Toughest Competition

This resume and its subsequent updates have been so successful, its owner refers to it as the "Magic Resume." It has achieved its goal three times in a row: first in attaining an in-house competitive promotion with a whopping 36 percent increase in salary, next in obtaining an even *more* lucrative position and, most recently, in securing comparable relocation employment in a constrained market—all on the first try!

The magic in this resume was conjured up by describing the job seeker's "experiences and accomplishments in an objective, succinct and interesting manner," says Jeannie Carlson. These nine rules that Carlson conveys to her clients were followed.

1. Eliminate the "I-me-my" focus by writing the resume in the first person implied. This facilitates a straightforward presentation without impressions of egotism or false modesty.
2. Initiate sentences with action verbs. This moves along otherwise mundane details and duties with sparkle.
3. Take inventory of specific accomplishments, identifying and itemizing them separately from duties and responsibilities. This will show you can do more for the employer than the next person.
4. Avoid using the same verbs and phrases over and over. If several consecutive sentences begin with "Developed and implemented," for instance, there is a good chance subsequent sentences will be skipped over as repetitive.
5. Be concise. Focus on developing an inverted pyramid of the last 10 years' experience, saying more about current employment.
6. Use terminology appropriate to your profession. Incorporate industry buzzwords, but be subtle so that you don't appear pretentious.
7. Use words that convey your personality to add individuality to an otherwise cookie-cutter document. An innovative person might say he "pioneered" rather than "developed."
8. Prioritize information within each job description to increase your chances that the reader will scan the most important items first.
9. Print the resume on good quality bond using bold and standard typefaces to highlight the resume and boost its overall appearance.

Jeannie Carlson
President, Viking Communications, Inc.

Jeannie Carlson is the president of Viking Communications, Inc., a professional writing company she founded in St. Petersburg, Fla., in 1987. Recognized in the Marquis edition of *Who's Who in America*, she has garnered numerous awards in fiction and nonfiction writing with multiple freelance credits in newspapers, periodicals and books nationwide. Her articles on resume preparation have appeared in such publications as the *St. Petersburg Times*, *Equal Opportunity Magazine* and *Veterans Chronicle*. Distinguished as ABI Woman of the Year for 1995 and 1996, she is frequently recruited to provide resume consultations at job fairs in the Tampa Bay area.

Note: The resume was printed as a fold-open four-part brochure. The original cover page (which does not appear here) had the client's name, address and phone number as well as an objective presented as an overview of expertise.

PROFILE
Dedicated and meticulous health care professional with fifteen years proven record of accomplishments in personnel management, business functions and behavioral science. Proficient in planning, developing, supervising and implementing diversified policies, programs and procedures for optimum productivity and cost efficiency. Adept at both oral and written communication skills, interacting effectively with individuals from all walks of life. Excel at directing and motivating a cohesive staff in the successful attainment of corporate objectives.

EDUCATION
Master of Science in Counseling-Completed: 10 Credit Hours Towards Degree
TROY STATE UNIVERSITY, Dothan, Alabama

Bachelor of Arts in Psychology - Degree Conferred: 1983
RANDOLPH-MACON WOMAN'S COLLEGE, Lynchburg, Virginia

Health Care Management & Procedural Training (St. Petersburg, FL)
ST. JOSEPH'S-ST. ANTHONY'S HEALTH SYSTEM: 1994-Present (44 Hrs.)
-WORDPERFECT
-LOTUS 1-2-3
-FINANCIAL APPLICATIONS
-MISSION VALUES
-INTERVIEWING STANDARDS
-MEDICARE/MEDICAID

Department of Human Resources Training
STATE OF GEORGIA: 1977-1978 (98 Hours)
-CONFIDENTIALITY WORKSHOP
-ADULT WORKSHOPS & WORK ACTIVITIES I & I
-MINIMUM STANDARDS REVISIONS
-WORKSHOP ORGANIZATION
-NORMALIZATION WORKSHOP
-MANAGEMENT IN STATE GOVERNMENT, LEVEL I

Hypnoanalysis for Positive Sexual Functioning
SOCIETY OF MEDICAL HYPNOANALYSTS, Tampa, Florida
Certification Conferred: November 1982 (24 Hours)

Introduction to Neurolinguistic Programming (Mobile, Alabama)
Received One C.E. Credit: June 1982 (16 Hours)

How to Communicate Under Pressure; Dealing With Difficult People
ENTERPRISE STATE JUNIOR COLLEGE, Enterprise, Alabama
Received One C.E. Credit: April 1982 (16 Hours)

Instructors Course in Standard Emergency First Aid
& Standard Emergency First Aid Course
AMERICAN RED CROSS, Savannah, Georgia
Certifications Conferred: June 1978 (8 Hours) & February 1978 (8 Hours)

Behavior Task Analysis Workshop
GEORGIA SOUTHERN COLLEGE, Statesboro, Georgia
Received One C.E. Credit: May 1978 (10 Hours)

CIVIC
*Alumnae Representative, Randolph-Macon Woman's College: 9/96-Present
*Board Member, Largo High School Band of Gold: 8/96-Present
*Volunteer, Largo High School Band of Gold Boosters: 11/95-Present

CAREER HISTORY

Business Office Supervisor: January 1994 - Present
ST. JOSEPH'S-ST. ANTHONY'S HEALTH SYSTEM, St. Petersburg, Florida
-Impact all patient account management functions for existing and new Home Health clients. Provide management and client support via constructing management reports and researching billing and collection issues. Execute backup of department staff on all client functions. Select, train, evaluate, develop and direct Collection, Billing and Clerical personnel, managing a staff of 6-12 employees. Actuate on-site computer hardware/software support. Enhance team effort and create a professional environment in accordance with mission values. Establish compliance with departmental policies and procedures in pursuit of continuous value improvement, human resources, infection control, safety, and environmental standards. Evolve policies and controls to insure the timely, accurate and complete processing of all Agency billing. Effect follow-up on unpaid accounts. Conduct ongoing training on third party reimbursement and patient collection issues. Document AR trends, routine and otherwise to assist in compilation of monthly department activity report. Report directly to the Financial Director.
* Instrumental in facilitating transition during the merger of St. Anthony's with St. Joseph's, 1994.
* Act as liaison/troubleshooter/trainer for all computer conversions to Delta Health Systems on the Novell Network.
* Precipitated continuity and high standards of performance throughout staff fluctuations and restructuring.
* Volunteered at St. Anthony's Triathlon annual event, 1995 and 1997.

Business Office Manager: July 1992 - August 1993
CHARTER WOODS HOSPITAL, Dothan, Alabama
-Directed and managed the Business Office activities of a 75-bed Psychiatric Hospital, encompassing all day-to-day admissions, billing and collections functions, maximizing the hospital's financial position. Supervised the Admissions, Billing and Collections staff, including hiring, orienting, training, monitoring, evaluating and counseling employees. Established and maintained effective interdepartmental relationships with Needs Assessment, Utilization Review, Medical Records, and clinical services departments. Maintained multiple claims filed logs, reviewed daily reports and accounts receivable documentation, oversaw updating and posting, and made recommendations to the Controller for further account handling.
* Exceeded corporate accounts receivable management cash collection goal for all quarters, resulting in receiving Certificates of Achievement for Outstanding Accounts Receivable Management.
* Achieved status in the Top 10 Hospitals with the lowest Accounts Receivable days for the last 2 quarters.

Business Office Manager: May 1988 - July 1992
HUMANA HOSPITAL - ENTERPRISE, Enterprise, Alabama
-Managed a staff of 25 personnel in the daily Business Office operations of a 135-bed Medical-Surgical Hospital. Supervised and coordinated all activities involving the Admissions, Billing, Collections, Switchboard and Front Cashier departments. Accountable for all Accounts Receivable, Billing and Collections outcome. Utilized the MED A system for Medicare billings. Dealt with bankruptcy litigation, analyzed and authorized legal suits, and represented the company in contested legal suits.
* Reduced bad debt in the first 2 months to below corporate goal.
* Introduced and implemented cross-training of department personnel.
* Created and implemented an effective reorganization plan for the Business Office to facilitate work flow in accordance with employee cutbacks.
* Developed New Task Oriented Employee Job Descriptions.
* Promoted from Insurance Billing Clerk to Admission Supervisor (7/89) to Business Office Manager (12/91).

(OVER)

Behavior Education Instructor: February 1986 - August 1987
NUTRI/SYSTEM WEIGHT LOSS CENTER, Dothan, Alabama
-Scheduled and presented all weight loss classes and performed client evaluations of eating behaviors. Taught classes in Positive Self Thought and Image, Thought Focusing, Relaxation, Exercise, Nutrition, Assertiveness, and Motivation. Took blood pressures, weighed clients, measured and supervised client compliance with food program. Performed inventory control, fee collection, assembly and charging of client orders, and booking consultation appointments.
* Served as Office Manager in her absence.
* Compiled monthly newsletter.
* Traveled to other locations to service clients in more remote areas.

Registrar/Instructor/Owner: May 1982-May 1986
ENTERPRISE LAMAZE CHILDBIRTH EDUCATION CTR., Enterprise, AL
-Responsible for operations management of Lamaze Childbirth Education Program. Performed records management, including accounts payable and accounts receivable. Promoted the business via advertising flyers, newspaper and television announcements. Acted as Instructor, selecting appropriate visual and auditory aids, presenting material, arranging guest speakers, coordinating and conducting hospital labor and delivery room tours, and providing individual instruction to couples. As Registrar, provided course information, collected fees, and assigned instructors to couples.
* Promoted from Registrar to Instructor, May 1983.
* Purchased business from owner, June 1983.

Assistant/Office Manager: September 1981 - September 1985
ENTERPRISE MEDICAL CLINIC, Enterprise, Alabama
-Assisted and managed the Behavioral Medicine Office of a Physician and Licensed Professional Counselor. Scheduled appointments, screened patients, set up patient accounts, collected payments, and handled inventory. Maintained and organized files, video and cassette tape libraries and patient handouts. Submitted and expedited patient insurance form documentation. Supervised one employee, trained new employees, handled scheduling, and coordinated work flow.
* Substituted for the Pediatric Nurse in her absence.
* Created patient handouts.

Instructor Supervisor (Instructor II): September 1977-September 1978
STATE OF GEORGIA MERIT SYSTEM, DEPT. OF HUMAN RESOURCES
Riceboro, Georgia
-Supervised 7 instructors and instructor aids of retarded and handicapped children and adults. Assured the proper maintenance of student records as well as the quality and suitability of the curriculum. Conducted inservice training to staff as required by the state of Georgia. Monitored and coordinated time worked, comp time and substitute instructors. Assumed the responsibilities of Center Bus Driver as needed. Obtained work contracts, performed time studies, arranged for and accompanied clients on health service trips, and traveled throughout Georgia for workshops and meetings.
* Advanced from Instructor to Instructor Supervisor after 9 months.
* Designed new adult workshops and activities.
* Organized and directed the local Special Olympics between counties for approximately 100 participants.